What's in a Name?

ISBN: 978-1-60962-139-1

Printed by UNL Printing.

Copies may be purchased from Amazon.com and Lulu.com.

Art from canva.com and flaticon.com.

What's in a Name?
An Anthology

PupCup Publishing

Edited by:
Managing Editor- Rachael Wakefield
Acquisitions Editor- Evelyn Koch
Copy Editor- Nick Niendorf
Design Director- Morgan Gassert
Marketing Director- Natalie Albracht

Table of Contents

Introduction

The question of the power and influence a name holds has been explored in a myriad of stories from Shakespeare's *Romeo and Juliet* to Walt Disney's *The Lion King*. A name is part of one's identity. While some go by a nickname and others take legal measures to change their name, the existence of the original name is never erased, merely covered up, like a mask. Just as there are many reasons for donning a mask, there are many reasons why someone would choose to hide their name, even when choosing to publish their work. For some, like Benjamin Franklin, this mask is merely a costume, one that allows him to enter a different world for a bit, but he can take it off as he pleases. For others, the mask is a disguise necessary for survival, whether that survival be in their everyday lives or the literary industry. In the male-dominated society of the nineteenth century, the Brontë sisters could only gain entry to that world of respect and high regard as Currer, Ellis, and Acton Bell. Still others, like Samuel Clemens, wear that mask so often that it blends to their face, leaving their legacy under their pseudonym, such as Clemens did with his pen name Mark Twain.

The first half of this anthology, "Alter Ego," chooses to focus on authors who used their pseudonyms as an alter ego. This alter ego allowed them to create a different identity to separate their work from their public appearance. Just as one can create and decorate a mask with various materials, the pseudonymous author carefully crafts their alter ego. Some, such as Anton Chekhov, create multiple pseudonyms, different masks for different stories or situations. Some choose slight variations of their given names, while others choose a vastly different *nom de plume*. Yet, all the same, they have forged a new identity of themselves that can live on paper.

The selection of works in the second half of this anthology, "That's What (S)he Said," focuses on authors who not only needed to create a new identity, but also needed to hide their real identity, particularly their gender. Many times, the authors never explicitly stated the intended gender of the pseudonym, however, a stereotypically male (or in one case, female) name was enough to trick a publisher or reader into letting a work reach its desired audience. Frequently, for female authors who publish with male pseudonyms, this desired audience can be having any audience at all. While women's empowerment movements continue to make strides, female authors sometimes still choose to publish under a man's name in order to give their work more exposure and literary clout.

These thirteen pieces selected are certainly not an extensive list of all pseudonymous works. In fact, there may be many pieces that fit under this category that no one is aware of, simply because the author died having never been unmasked, the author's true identity remains a mystery—one that may always go unsolved since no one is aware of the mystery in the first place. These authors' pseudonyms allowed them to live double lives, even if one of those lives was only in a world of fiction. Whether an author was ultimately remembered for their original name or their pseudonym, no matter their motivation, no matter the number of works they published under their pseudonym, they all sought one thing: a new identity

Section 1:
Alter Ego

AE—George William Russell

George William Russell, popularly known as Æ, was born on April 10th, 1867 in Lurgan, Ireland. Russell was well-educated, and attended Dublin's Metropolitan School of Art in the 1880s, where he befriended the Irish poet, William Butler Yeats. He published his first piece, a collection of poems, in 1894 and gained credibility as a writer in the Irish literary community. Russell penned his works under the pseudonym of Æ, after his publisher convinced him to shorten Russell's original suggestion, Æon. Russell worked as a clerk for a period of time after school, and then become a prominent member of an Irish collectivist society. He was politically active throughout his life, and was renowned for his generosity and ability to mend relationships between his contemporaries. While eventually overshadowed by Yeats, Russell was held in equal esteem as him while alive. Russell died on July 17, 1935 in Bournemouth, England.

"Alter Ego"

ALL the morn a spirit gay
Breathes within my heart a rhyme,
'Tis but hide and seek we play
In and out the courts of time.

Fairy lover, when my feet
Through the tangled woodland go,
'Tis thy sunny fingers fleet
Fleck the fire dews to and fro.

In the moonlight grows a smile
Mid its rays of dusty pearl—
'Tis but hide and seek the while,
As some frolic boy and girl.

When I fade into the deep
Some mysterious radiance showers
From the jewel-heart of sleep
Through the veil of darkened hours.

Where the ring of twilight gleams
Round the sanctuary wrought,
Whispers haunt me—in my dreams
We are one yet know it not.

Some for beauty follow long
Flying traces; some there be
Seek thee only for a song:
I to lose myself in thee.

Boz—Charles Dickens

Charles Dickens, also known as "Boz," was born on February 7, 1812 in Portsmouth, England. Dickens was raised alongside seven siblings and their family moved frequently throughout his childhood. He read incessantly during his childhood, and would later use many of the settings and personalities present throughout his adolescence in his novels. Dickens published his first story, a comedic sketch, in 1933. He continued to write short pieces for popular English newspapers, eventually attaching the pseudonym "Boz" to them beginning in 1834. These works culminated in *Sketches by Boz*, a collection of stories published in 1836 which propelled Dickens to fame. He published his first novel, *The Pickwick Papers*, that same year, and *Oliver Twist* in 1838. Dickens went on to become one of the most important writers of the nineteenth century, producing works such as *A Christmas Carol, A Tale of Two Cities,* and *Great Expectations*. He died on June 8, 1870.

Sketches by Boz
CHAPTER I—THE BEADLE. THE PARISH ENGINE. THE SCHOOLMASTER

How much is conveyed in those two short words—'The Parish!' And with how many tales of distress and misery, of broken fortune and ruined hopes, too often of unrelieved wretchedness and successful knavery, are they associated! A poor man, with small earnings, and a large family, just manages to live on from hand to mouth, and to procure food from day to day; he has barely sufficient to satisfy the present cravings of nature, and can take no heed of the future. His taxes are in arrear, quarter-day passes by, another quarter-day arrives: he can procure no more quarter for himself, and is summoned by—the parish. His goods are distrained, his children are crying with cold and hunger, and the very bed on which his sick wife is lying, is dragged from beneath her. What can he do? To whom is he to apply for relief? To private charity? To benevolent individuals? Certainly not—there is his parish. There are the parish vestry, the parish infirmary, the parish surgeon, the parish officers, the parish beadle. Excellent institutions, and gentle, kind-hearted men. The woman dies—she is buried by the parish. The children have no protector—they are taken care of by the parish. The man first neglects, and afterwards cannot obtain, work—he is relieved by the parish; and when distress and drunkenness have done their work upon him, he is maintained, a harmless babbling idiot, in the parish asylum.

The parish beadle is one of the most, perhaps the most, important member of the local administration. He is not so well off as the churchwardens, certainly, nor is he so learned as the vestry-clerk, nor does he order things quite so much his own way as either of them. But his power is very great, notwithstanding; and the dignity of his office is never impaired by the absence of efforts on his part to maintain it. The beadle of our parish is a splendid fellow. It is quite delightful to hear him, as he explains the state of the existing poor laws to the deaf old women in the board-room passage on business nights; and to hear what he said to the senior churchwarden, and what the senior churchwarden said to him; and what 'we' (the beadle and the other gentlemen) came to the determination of doing. A miserable-looking woman is called into the boardroom, and represents a case of extreme destitution, affecting herself—a widow, with six small children. 'Where do you live?' inquires one of the overseers. 'I rents a two-pair back, gentlemen, at Mrs. Brown's, Number 3, Little King William's-alley, which has lived there this fifteen year, and knows me to be very hard-working and industrious, and when my poor husband was alive, gentlemen, as died in the hospital'—'Well, well,' interrupts the overseer, taking a note of the address, 'I'll send Simmons, the beadle, to-morrow morning, to ascertain whether your story is correct; and if so, I suppose you must have an order into the House—Simmons, go to this woman's the first thing to-morrow morning, will you?' Simmons bows assent, and ushers the woman out. Her previous admiration of 'the board' (who all sit behind great books, and with their hats on) fades into nothing before her respect for her lace-trimmed conductor; and her account of what has passed inside, increases—if that be possible—the marks of respect, shown by the assembled crowd, to that solemn functionary. As to taking out a summons, it's quite a hopeless case if Simmons attends it, on behalf of the parish. He knows all the titles of the Lord Mayor by heart; states the case without a single stammer: and it is even reported that on one occasion he ventured to make a joke, which the Lord Mayor's head footman (who happened to be present) afterwards told an intimate friend, confidentially, was almost equal to one of Mr. Hobler's.

See him again on Sunday in his state-coat and cocked-hat, with a large-headed staff for show in his left hand, and a small cane for use in his right. How pompously he marshals the children into their places! and how demurely the little urchins look at him askance as he surveys them when they are all seated, with a glare of the eye peculiar to beadles! The churchwardens and overseers being duly installed in their curtained pews, he seats himself on a mahogany bracket, erected expressly for him at the top of the aisle, and divides his attention between his prayer-book and the boys. Suddenly, just at the commencement of the communion service, when the whole congregation is hushed into a profound silence, broken only by the voice of the officiating clergyman, a penny is heard to ring on the stone floor of the aisle with astounding clearness. Observe the generalship of the beadle. His involuntary look of horror is instantly changed into one of perfect indifference, as if he were the only person present who had not heard the noise. The artifice succeeds. After putting forth his right leg now and then, as a feeler, the victim who dropped the money ventures to make one or two distinct dives after it; and the beadle, gliding softly round, salutes his little round head, when it again appears above the seat, with divers double knocks, administered with the cane before noticed, to the intense delight of three young men in an adjacent pew, who cough violently at intervals until the conclusion of the sermon.

Such are a few traits of the importance and gravity of a parish beadle—a gravity which has never been disturbed in any case that has come under our observation, except when the services of that particularly useful machine, a parish fire-engine, are required: then indeed all is bustle. Two little boys run to the beadle as fast as their legs will carry them, and report from their own personal observation that some neighbouring chimney is on fire; the engine is hastily got out, and a plentiful supply of boys being obtained, and harnessed to it with ropes, away they rattle over the pavement, the beadle, running—we do not exaggerate—running at the side, until they arrive at some house, smelling strongly of soot, at the door of which the beadle knocks with considerable gravity for half-an-hour. No attention being paid to these manual applications, and the turn-cock having turned on the water, the engine turns off amidst the shouts of the boys; it pulls up once more at the work-house, and the beadle 'pulls up' the unfortunate householder next day, for the amount of his legal reward. We never saw a parish engine at a regular fire but once. It came up in gallant style— three miles and a half an hour, at least; there was a capital supply of water, and it was first on the spot. Bang went the pumps—the people cheered—the beadle perspired profusely; but it was unfortunately discovered, just as they were going to put the fire out, that nobody understood the process by which the engine was filled with water; and that eighteen boys, and a man, had exhausted themselves in pumping for twenty minutes, without producing the slightest effect!

The personages next in importance to the beadle, are the master of the workhouse and the parish schoolmaster. The vestry-clerk, as everybody knows, is a short, pudgy little man, in black, with a thick gold watch-chain of considerable length, terminating in two large seals and a key. He is an attorney, and generally in a bustle; at no time more so, than when he is hurrying to some parochial meeting, with his gloves crumpled up in one hand, and a large red book under the other arm. As to the churchwardens and overseers, we exclude them altogether, because all we know of them is, that they are usually respectable tradesmen, who wear hats with brims inclined to flatness, and who occasionally testify in gilt letters on a blue ground, in some conspicuous part of the church, to the important fact of a gallery having being enlarged and beautified, or an organ rebuilt.

The master of the workhouse is not, in our parish—nor is he usually in any other—one of that class of men the better part of whose existence has passed away, and who drag out the remainder in some inferior situation, with just enough thought of the past, to feel degraded by, and discontented with the present. We are unable to guess precisely to our own satisfaction what station the man can have occupied before; we should think he had been an inferior sort of attorney's clerk, or else the master of a national school—whatever he was, it is clear his present position is a change for the better. His income is small certainly, as the rusty black coat and threadbare velvet collar demonstrate: but then he lives free of house-rent, has a limited allowance of coals and candles, and an almost unlimited allowance of authority in his petty kingdom. He is a tall, thin, bony man; always wears shoes and black cotton stockings with his surtout; and eyes you, as you pass his parlour-window, as if he wished you were a pauper, just to give you a specimen of his power. He is an admirable specimen of a small tyrant: morose, brutish, and ill-tempered; bullying to his inferiors, cringing to his superiors, and jealous of the influence and authority of the beadle.

Our schoolmaster is just the very reverse of this amiable official. He has been one of those men one occasionally hears of, on whom misfortune seems to have set her mark; nothing he ever did, or was concerned in, appears to have prospered. A rich old relation who had brought him up, and openly announced his intention of providing for him, left him 10,000l. in his will, and revoked the bequest in a codicil. Thus unexpectedly reduced to the necessity of providing for himself, he procured a situation in a public office. The young clerks below him, died off as if there were a plague among them; but the old fellows over his head, for the reversion of whose places he was anxiously waiting, lived on and on, as if they were immortal. He speculated and lost. He speculated again and won—but never got his money. His talents were great; his disposition, easy, generous and liberal. His friends profited by the one, and abused the other. Loss succeeded loss; misfortune crowded on misfortune; each successive day brought him nearer the verge of hopeless penury, and the quondam friends who had been warmest in their professions, grew strangely cold and indifferent. He had children whom he loved, and a wife on whom he doted. The former turned their backs on him; the latter died broken-hearted. He went with the stream—it had ever been his failing, and he had not courage sufficient to bear up against so many shocks—he had never cared for himself, and the only being who had cared for him, in his poverty and distress, was spared to him no longer. It was at this period that he applied for parochial relief. Some kind-hearted man who had known him in happier times, chanced to be churchwarden that year, and through his interest he was appointed to his present situation.

He is an old man now. Of the many who once crowded round him in all the hollow friendship of boon-companionship, some have died, some have fallen like himself, some have prospered—all have forgotten him. Time and misfortune have mercifully been permitted to impair his memory, and use has habituated him to his present condition. Meek, uncomplaining, and zealous in the discharge of his duties, he has been allowed to hold his situation long beyond the usual period; and he will no doubt continue to hold it, until infirmity renders him incapable, or death releases him. As the grey-headed old man feebly paces up and down the sunny side of the little court-yard between school hours, it would be difficult, indeed, for the most intimate of his former friends to recognise their once gay and happy associate, in the person of the Pauper Schoolmaster.

Lewis Carroll—Charles Lutwidge Dodgson

Charles Lutwidge Dodgson, better known as "Lewis Carroll," was born on January 27, 1832 in Cheshire, England. Dodgson spent much of his early life devoting himself to the Oxford Church as a scholar and a teacher. He began writing short stories and poetry at a young age, many of which were published in small magazines and later national publications. His first use of the pseudonym "Lewis Carroll" was in 1856 when he submitted a romantic poem to *The Train*. At the insistence of his colleague's young daughter, Dodgson turned a story he had told to her into a manuscript which he later submitted to a publisher. The story was published in 1865 as *Alice's Adventures in Wonderland*, which launched Dodgson into both commercial and critical success. He later went on to produce a sequel, as well as a myriad of other popular works. Throughout his life, he took up interests in photography, engineering, and mathematics. He died of pneumonia after a bout with influenza on January 14, 1898.

THE HUNTING OF THE SNARK
an Agony, in Eight Fits

PREFACE

If--and the thing is wildly possible--the charge of writing nonsense were ever brought against the author of this brief but instructive poem, it would be based, I feel convinced, on the line (in p.4)

"Then the bowsprit got mixed with the rudder sometimes."

In view of this painful possibility, I will not (as I might) appeal indignantly to my other writings as a proof that I am incapable of such a deed: I will not (as I might) point to the strong moral purpose of this poem itself, to the arithmetical principles so cautiously inculcated in it, or to its noble teachings in Natural History--I will take the more prosaic course of simply explaining how it happened.

The Bellman, who was almost morbidly sensitive about appearances, used to have the bowsprit unshipped once or twice a week to be revarnished, and it more than once happened, when the time came for replacing it, that no one on board could remember which end of the ship it belonged to. They knew it was not of the slightest use to appeal to the Bellman about it--he would only refer to his Naval Code, and read out in pathetic tones Admiralty Instructions which none of them had ever been able to understand--so it generally ended in its being fastened on, anyhow, across the rudder. The helmsman used to stand by with tears in his eyes; he knew it was all wrong, but alas! Rule 42 of the Code, "No one shall speak to the Man at the Helm," had been completed by the Bellman himself with the words "and the Man at the Helm shall speak to no one." So remonstrance was impossible, and no steering could be done till the next varnishing day. During these bewildering intervals the ship usually sailed backwards.

As this poem is to some extent connected with the lay of the Jabberwock, let me take this opportunity of answering a question that has often been asked me, how to pronounce "slithy toves." The "i" in "slithy" is long, as in "writhe"; and "toves" is pronounced so as to rhyme with "groves." Again, the first "o" in "boro-goves" is pronounced like the "o" in "borrow." I have heard people try to give it the sound of the "o" in "worry". Such is Human Perversity.

This also seems a fitting occasion to notice the other hard words in that poem. Humpty-Dumpty's theory, of two meanings packed into one word like a portmanteau, seems to me the right explanation for all. For instance, take the two words "fuming" and "furious." Make up your mind that you will say both words, but leave it unsettled which you will first. Now open your mouth and speak. If your thoughts incline ever so little towards "fuming," you will say "fuming-furious;" if they turn, by even a hair's breadth, towards "furious," you will say "furious-fuming;" but if you have the rarest of gifts, a perfectly balanced mind, you will say "frumious."

Supposing that, when Pistol uttered the well-known words--
"Under which king, Bezonian? Speak or die!"

Justice Shallow had felt certain that it was either William or Richard, but had not been able to settle which, so that he could not possibly say either name before the other, can it be doubted that, rather than die, he would have gasped out "Rilchiam!"

Fit the First
THE LANDING

"Just the place for a Snark!" the Bellman cried,
    As he landed his crew with care;
Supporting each man on the top of the tide
    By a finger entwined in his hair.

"Just the place for a Snark! I have said it twice:
    That alone should encourage the crew.
Just the place for a Snark! I have said it thrice:
    What I tell you three times is true."

The crew was complete: it included a Boots--
    A maker of Bonnets and Hoods--
A Barrister, brought to arrange their disputes--
    And a Broker, to value their goods.

A Billiard-marker, whose skill was immense,
    Might perhaps have won more than his share--

But a Banker, engaged at enormous expense,
        Had the whole of their cash in his care.

There was also a Beaver, that paced on the deck,
        Or would sit making lace in the bow:
And had often (the Bellman said) saved them from wreck,
        Though none of the sailors knew how.

There was one who was famed for the number of things
        He forgot when he entered the ship:
His umbrella, his watch, all his jewels and rings,
        And the clothes he had bought for the trip.

He had forty-two boxes, all carefully packed,
        With his name painted clearly on each:
But, since he omitted to mention the fact,
        They were all left behind on the beach.

The loss of his clothes hardly mattered, because
        He had seven coats on when he came,
With three pairs of boots--but the worst of it was,
        He had wholly forgotten his name.

He would answer to "Hi!" or to any loud cry,
        Such as "Fry me!" or "Fritter my wig!"
To "What-you-may-call-um!" or "What-was-his-name!"
        But especially "Thing-um-a-jig!"

While, for those who preferred a more forcible word,
        He had different names from these:
His intimate friends called him "Candle-ends,"
        And his enemies "Toasted-cheese."

"His form is ungainly--his intellect small--"
        (So the Bellman would often remark)
"But his courage is perfect! And that, after all,
        Is the thing that one needs with a Snark."

He would joke with hyenas, returning their stare
        With an impudent wag of the head:
And he once went a walk, paw-in-paw, with a bear,
        "Just to keep up its spirits," he said.

He came as a Baker: but owned, when too late--

And it drove the poor Bellman half-mad--
He could only bake Bridecake--for which, I may state,
No materials were to be had.
The last of the crew needs especial remark,
Though he looked an incredible dunce:
He had just one idea--but, that one being "Snark,"
The good Bellman engaged him at once.

He came as a Butcher: but gravely declared,
When the ship had been sailing a week,
He could only kill Beavers. The Bellman looked scared,
And was almost too frightened to speak:

But at length he explained, in a tremulous tone,
There was only one Beaver on board;
And that was a tame one he had of his own,
Whose death would be deeply deplored.

The Beaver, who happened to hear the remark,
Protested, with tears in its eyes,
That not even the rapture of hunting the Snark
Could atone for that dismal surprise!

It strongly advised that the Butcher should be
Conveyed in a separate ship:
But the Bellman declared that would never agree
With the plans he had made for the trip:

Navigation was always a difficult art,
Though with only one ship and one bell:
And he feared he must really decline, for his part,
Undertaking another as well.

The Beaver's best course was, no doubt, to procure
A second-hand dagger-proof coat--
So the Baker advised it--and next, to insure
Its life in some Office of note:

This the Banker suggested, and offered for hire
(On moderate terms), or for sale,
Two excellent Policies, one Against Fire,
And one Against Damage From Hail.

Yet still, ever after that sorrowful day,

Whenever the Butcher was by,
The Beaver kept looking the opposite way,
And appeared unaccountably shy.

Fit the Second
THE BELLMAN'S SPEECH

The Bellman himself they all praised to the skies--
Such a carriage, such ease and such grace!
Such solemnity, too! One could see he was wise,
The moment one looked in his face!

He had bought a large map representing the sea,
Without the least vestige of land:
And the crew were much pleased when they found it to be
A map they could all understand.

"What's the good of Mercator's North Poles and Equators,
Tropics, Zones, and Meridian Lines?"
So the Bellman would cry: and the crew would reply
"They are merely conventional signs!

"Other maps are such shapes, with their islands and capes!
But we've got our brave Captain to thank:"
(So the crew would protest) "that he's bought us the best--
A perfect and absolute blank!"

This was charming, no doubt; but they shortly found out
That the Captain they trusted so well
Had only one notion for crossing the ocean,
And that was to tingle his bell.

He was thoughtful and grave--but the orders he gave
Were enough to bewilder a crew.
When he cried "Steer to starboard, but keep her head larboard!"
What on earth was the helmsman to do?

Then the bowsprit got mixed with the rudder sometimes:
A thing, as the Bellman remarked,
That frequently happens in tropical climes,
When a vessel is, so to speak, "snarked."
But the principal failing occurred in the sailing,

And the Bellman, perplexed and distressed,
Said he had hoped, at least, when the wind blew due East,
That the ship would not travel due West!

But the danger was past--they had landed at last,
With their boxes, portmanteaus, and bags:
Yet at first sight the crew were not pleased with the view,
Which consisted of chasms and crags.

The Bellman perceived that their spirits were low,
And repeated in musical tone
Some jokes he had kept for a season of woe--
But the crew would do nothing but groan.

He served out some grog with a liberal hand,
And bade them sit down on the beach:
And they could not but own that their Captain looked grand,
As he stood and delivered his speech.

"Friends, Romans, and countrymen, lend me your ears!"
(They were all of them fond of quotations:
So they drank to his health, and they gave him three cheers,
While he served out additional rations).

"We have sailed many months, we have sailed many weeks,
(Four weeks to the month you may mark),
But never as yet ('tis your Captain who speaks)
Have we caught the least glimpse of a Snark!

"We have sailed many weeks, we have sailed many days,
(Seven days to the week I allow),
But a Snark, on the which we might lovingly gaze,
We have never beheld till now!

"Come, listen, my men, while I tell you again
The five unmistakable marks
By which you may know, wheresoever you go,
The warranted genuine Snarks.

"Let us take them in order. The first is the taste,
Which is meagre and hollow, but crisp:
Like a coat that is rather too tight in the waist,
With a flavour of Will-o'-the-wisp.

"Its habit of getting up late you'll agree
That it carries too far, when I say
That it frequently breakfasts at five-o'clock tea,
And dines on the following day.
"The third is its slowness in taking a jest.
Should you happen to venture on one,
It will sigh like a thing that is deeply distressed:
And it always looks grave at a pun.

"The fourth is its fondness for bathing-machines,
Which is constantly carries about,
And believes that they add to the beauty of scenes--
A sentiment open to doubt.

"The fifth is ambition. It next will be right
To describe each particular batch:
Distinguishing those that have feathers, and bite,
And those that have whiskers, and scratch.

"For, although common Snarks do no manner of harm,
Yet, I feel it my duty to say,
Some are Boojums--" The Bellman broke off in alarm,
For the Baker had fainted away.

Fit the Third
THE BAKER'S TALE

They roused him with muffins--they roused him with ice--
They roused him with mustard and cress--
They roused him with jam and judicious advice--
They set him conundrums to guess.

When at length he sat up and was able to speak,
His sad story he offered to tell;
And the Bellman cried "Silence! Not even a shriek!"
And excitedly tingled his bell.

There was silence supreme! Not a shriek, not a scream,

Scarcely even a howl or a groan,
As the man they called "Ho!" told his story of woe
In an antediluvian tone.

"My father and mother were honest, though poor--"
"Skip all that!" cried the Bellman in haste.
"If it once becomes dark, there's no chance of a Snark--
We have hardly a minute to waste!"

"I skip forty years," said the Baker, in tears,
"And proceed without further remark
To the day when you took me aboard of your ship
To help you in hunting the Snark.

"A dear uncle of mine (after whom I was named)
Remarked, when I bade him farewell--"
"Oh, skip your dear uncle!" the Bellman exclaimed,
As he angrily tingled his bell.

"He remarked to me then," said that mildest of men,
"'If your Snark be a Snark, that is right:
Fetch it home by all means--you may serve it with greens,
And it's handy for striking a light.

"'You may seek it with thimbles--and seek it with care;
You may hunt it with forks and hope;
You may threaten its life with a railway-share;
You may charm it with smiles and soap--'"

("That's exactly the method," the Bellman bold
In a hasty parenthesis cried,
"That's exactly the way I have always been told
That the capture of Snarks should be tried!")

"'But oh, beamish nephew, beware of the day,
If your Snark be a Boojum! For then
You will softly and suddenly vanish away,
And never be met with again!'

"It is this, it is this that oppresses my soul,
When I think of my uncle's last words:
And my heart is like nothing so much as a bowl
Brimming over with quivering curds!

"It is this, it is this--" "We have had that before!"
The Bellman indignantly said.
And the Baker replied "Let me say it once more.
It is this, it is this that I dread!

"I engage with the Snark--every night after dark--
In a dreamy delirious fight:
I serve it with greens in those shadowy scenes,
And I use it for striking a light:

"But if ever I meet with a Boojum, that day,
In a moment (of this I am sure),
I shall softly and suddenly vanish away--
And the notion I cannot endure!"

Fit the Fourth
THE HUNTING

The Bellman looked huffish, and wrinkled his brow.
"If only you'd spoken before!
It's excessively awkward to mention it now,
With the Snark, so to speak, at the door!

"We should all of us grieve, as you well may believe,
If you never were met with again--
But surely, my man, when the voyage began,
You might have suggested it then?

"It's excessively awkward to mention it now--
As I think I've already remarked."
And the man they called "Hi!" replied, with a sigh,
"I informed you the day we embarked.

"You may charge me with murder--or want of sense--
(We are all of us weak at times):
But the slightest approach to a false pretence
Was never among my crimes!

"I said it in Hebrew--I said it in Dutch--
I said it in German and Greek:
But I wholly forgot (and it vexes me much)
That English is what you speak!"

"'Tis a pitiful tale," said the Bellman, whose face
Had grown longer at every word:
"But, now that you've stated the whole of your case,
More debate would be simply absurd.
"The rest of my speech" (he explained to his men)

"You shall hear when I've leisure to speak it.
But the Snark is at hand, let me tell you again!
'Tis your glorious duty to seek it!

"To seek it with thimbles, to seek it with care;
To pursue it with forks and hope;
To threaten its life with a railway-share;
To charm it with smiles and soap!

"For the Snark's a peculiar creature, that won't
Be caught in a commonplace way.
Do all that you know, and try all that you don't:
Not a chance must be wasted to-day!

"For England expects--I forbear to proceed:
'Tis a maxim tremendous, but trite:
And you'd best be unpacking the things that you need
To rig yourselves out for the fight."

Then the Banker endorsed a blank cheque (which he crossed),
And changed his loose silver for notes.
The Baker with care combed his whiskers and hair,
And shook the dust out of his coats.

The Boots and the Broker were sharpening a spade--
Each working the grindstone in turn:
But the Beaver went on making lace, and displayed
No interest in the concern:

Though the Barrister tried to appeal to its pride,
And vainly proceeded to cite
A number of cases, in which making laces
Had been proved an infringement of right.

The maker of Bonnets ferociously planned

A novel arrangement of bows:
While the Billiard-marker with quivering hand
Was chalking the tip of his nose.
But the Butcher turned nervous, and dressed himself fine,
With yellow kid gloves and a ruff--
Said he felt it exactly like going to dine,
Which the Bellman declared was all "stuff."

"Introduce me, now there's a good fellow," he said,
"If we happen to meet it together!"
And the Bellman, sagaciously nodding his head,
Said "That must depend on the weather."

The Beaver went simply galumphing about,
At seeing the Butcher so shy:
And even the Baker, though stupid and stout,
Made an effort to wink with one eye.

"Be a man!" said the Bellman in wrath, as he heard
The Butcher beginning to sob.
"Should we meet with a Jubjub, that desperate bird,
We shall need all our strength for the job!"

Fit the Fifth
THE BEAVER'S LESSON

They sought it with thimbles, they sought it with care;
They pursued it with forks and hope;
They threatened its life with a railway-share;
They charmed it with smiles and soap.

Then the Butcher contrived an ingenious plan
For making a separate sally;
And had fixed on a spot unfrequented by man,
A dismal and desolate valley.

But the very same plan to the Beaver occurred:
It had chosen the very same place:

Yet neither betrayed, by a sign or a word,
The disgust that appeared in his face.

Each thought he was thinking of nothing but "Snark"
And the glorious work of the day;
And each tried to pretend that he did not remark
That the other was going that way.

But the valley grew narrow and narrower still,
And the evening got darker and colder,
Till (merely from nervousness, not from goodwill)
They marched along shoulder to shoulder.
Then a scream, shrill and high, rent the shuddering sky,
And they knew that some danger was near:
The Beaver turned pale to the tip of its tail,
And even the Butcher felt queer.

He thought of his childhood, left far far behind--
That blissful and innocent state--
The sound so exactly recalled to his mind
A pencil that squeaks on a slate!

"'Tis the voice of the Jubjub!" he suddenly cried.
(This man, that they used to call "Dunce.")
"As the Bellman would tell you," he added with pride,
"I have uttered that sentiment once.

"'Tis the note of the Jubjub! Keep count, I entreat;
You will find I have told it you twice.
'Tis the song of the Jubjub! The proof is complete,
If only I've stated it thrice."

The Beaver had counted with scrupulous care,
Attending to every word:
But it fairly lost heart, and outgrabe in despair,
When the third repetition occurred.
It felt that, in spite of all possible pains,
It had somehow contrived to lose count,
And the only thing now was to rack its poor brains
By reckoning up the amount.

"Two added to one--if that could but be done,"
It said, "with one's fingers and thumbs!"
Recollecting with tears how, in earlier years,

It had taken no pains with its sums.

"The thing can be done," said the Butcher, "I think.
The thing must be done, I am sure.
The thing shall be done! Bring me paper and ink,
The best there is time to procure."

The Beaver brought paper, portfolio, pens,
And ink in unfailing supplies:
While strange creepy creatures came out of their dens,
And watched them with wondering eyes.

So engrossed was the Butcher, he heeded them not,
As he wrote with a pen in each hand,
And explained all the while in a popular style
Which the Beaver could well understand.

"Taking Three as the subject to reason about--
A convenient number to state--
We add Seven, and Ten, and then multiply out
By One Thousand diminished by Eight.

"The result we proceed to divide, as you see,
By Nine Hundred and Ninety Two:
Then subtract Seventeen, and the answer must be
Exactly and perfectly true.

"The method employed I would gladly explain,
While I have it so clear in my head,
If I had but the time and you had but the brain--
But much yet remains to be said.

"In one moment I've seen what has hitherto been
Enveloped in absolute mystery,
And without extra charge I will give you at large
A Lesson in Natural History."

In his genial way he proceeded to say
(Forgetting all laws of propriety,
And that giving instruction, without introduction,
Would have caused quite a thrill in Society),

"As to temper the Jubjub's a desperate bird,
Since it lives in perpetual passion:

Its taste in costume is entirely absurd--
It is ages ahead of the fashion:

"But it knows any friend it has met once before:
It never will look at a bribe:
And in charity-meetings it stands at the door,
And collects--though it does not subscribe.

"Its' flavour when cooked is more exquisite far
Than mutton, or oysters, or eggs:
(Some think it keeps best in an ivory jar,
And some, in mahogany kegs:)
"You boil it in sawdust: you salt it in glue:
You condense it with locusts and tape:
Still keeping one principal object in view--
To preserve its symmetrical shape."

The Butcher would gladly have talked till next day,
But he felt that the lesson must end,
And he wept with delight in attempting to say
He considered the Beaver his friend.
While the Beaver confessed, with affectionate looks
More eloquent even than tears,
It had learned in ten minutes far more than all books
Would have taught it in seventy years.

They returned hand-in-hand, and the Bellman, unmanned
(For a moment) with noble emotion,
Said "This amply repays all the wearisome days
We have spent on the billowy ocean!"

Such friends, as the Beaver and Butcher became,
Have seldom if ever been known;
In winter or summer, 'twas always the same--
You could never meet either alone.

And when quarrels arose--as one frequently finds
Quarrels will, spite of every endeavour--
The song of the Jubjub recurred to their minds,
And cemented their friendship for ever!

Fit the Sixth
THE BARRISTER'S DREAM

They sought it with thimbles, they sought it with care;
They pursued it with forks and hope;
They threatened its life with a railway-share;
They charmed it with smiles and soap.

But the Barrister, weary of proving in vain
That the Beaver's lace-making was wrong,
Fell asleep, and in dreams saw the creature quite plain
That his fancy had dwelt on so long.

He dreamed that he stood in a shadowy Court,
Where the Snark, with a glass in its eye,
Dressed in gown, bands, and wig, was defending a pig
On the charge of deserting its sty.

The Witnesses proved, without error or flaw,
That the sty was deserted when found:
And the Judge kept explaining the state of the law
In a soft under-current of sound.

The indictment had never been clearly expressed,
And it seemed that the Snark had begun,
And had spoken three hours, before any one guessed
What the pig was supposed to have done.

The Jury had each formed a different view
(Long before the indictment was read),
And they all spoke at once, so that none of them knew
One word that the others had said.

"You must know--" said the Judge: but the Snark exclaimed "Fudge!"
That statute is obsolete quite!
Let me tell you, my friends, the whole question depends

On an ancient manorial right.

"In the matter of Treason the pig would appear
To have aided, but scarcely abetted:
While the charge of Insolvency fails, it is clear,
If you grant the plea 'never indebted.'

"The fact of Desertion I will not dispute;
But its guilt, as I trust, is removed
(So far as related to the costs of this suit)
By the Alibi which has been proved.

"My poor client's fate now depends on your votes."
Here the speaker sat down in his place,
And directed the Judge to refer to his notes
And briefly to sum up the case.

But the Judge said he never had summed up before;
So the Snark undertook it instead,
And summed it so well that it came to far more
Than the Witnesses ever had said!

When the verdict was called for, the Jury declined,
As the word was so puzzling to spell;
But they ventured to hope that the Snark wouldn't mind
Undertaking that duty as well.

So the Snark found the verdict, although, as it owned,
It was spent with the toils of the day:
When it said the word "GUILTY!" the Jury all groaned,
And some of them fainted away.

Then the Snark pronounced sentence, the Judge being quite
Too nervous to utter a word:
When it rose to its feet, there was silence like night,
And the fall of a pin might be heard.

"Transportation for life" was the sentence it gave,
"And then to be fined forty pound."
The Jury all cheered, though the Judge said he feared
That the phrase was not legally sound.

But their wild exultation was suddenly checked
When the jailer informed them, with tears,

Such a sentence would have not the slightest effect,
As the pig had been dead for some years.

The Judge left the Court, looking deeply disgusted:
But the Snark, though a little aghast,
As the lawyer to whom the defense was entrusted,
Went bellowing on to the last.

Thus the Barrister dreamed, while the bellowing seemed
To grow every moment more clear:
Till he woke to the knell of a furious bell,
Which the Bellman rang close at his ear.

Fit the Seventh
THE BANKER'S FATE

They sought it with thimbles, they sought it with care;
They pursued it with forks and hope;
They threatened its life with a railway-share;
They charmed it with smiles and soap.

And the Banker, inspired with a courage so new
It was matter for general remark,
Rushed madly ahead and was lost to their view
In his zeal to discover the Snark

But while he was seeking with thimbles and care,
A Bandersnatch swiftly drew nigh
And grabbed at the Banker, who shrieked in despair,
For he knew it was useless to fly.

He offered large discount--he offered a cheque
(Drawn "to bearer") for seven-pounds-ten:
But the Bandersnatch merely extended its neck
And grabbed at the Banker again.

Without rest or pause--while those frumious jaws
Went savagely snapping around--
He skipped and he hopped, and he floundered and flopped,
Till fainting he fell to the ground.

The Bandersnatch fled as the others appeared
Led on by that fear-stricken yell:
And the Bellman remarked "It is just as I feared!"
And solemnly tolled on his bell.

He was black in the face, and they scarcely could trace
The least likeness to what he had been:
While so great was his fright that his waistcoat turned white--
A wonderful thing to be seen!

To the horror of all who were present that day.
He uprose in full evening dress,
And with senseless grimaces endeavoured to say
What his tongue could no longer express.

Down he sank in a chair--ran his hands through his hair--
And chanted in mimsiest tones
Words whose utter inanity proved his insanity,
While he rattled a couple of bones.

"Leave him here to his fate--it is getting so late!"
The Bellman exclaimed in a fright.
"We have lost half the day. Any further delay,
And we sha'nt catch a Snark before night!"

Fit the Eighth
THE VANISHING

They sought it with thimbles, they sought it with care;
They pursued it with forks and hope;
They threatened its life with a railway-share;
They charmed it with smiles and soap.
They shuddered to think that the chase might fail,
And the Beaver, excited at last,
Went bounding along on the tip of its tail,
For the daylight was nearly past.

"There is Thingumbob shouting!" the Bellman said,

"He is shouting like mad, only hark!
He is waving his hands, he is wagging his head,
He has certainly found a Snark!"

They gazed in delight, while the Butcher exclaimed
"He was always a desperate wag!"
They beheld him--their Baker--their hero unnamed--
On the top of a neighboring crag.

Erect and sublime, for one moment of time.
In the next, that wild figure they saw
(As if stung by a spasm) plunge into a chasm,
While they waited and listened in awe.

"It's a Snark!" was the sound that first came to their ears,
And seemed almost too good to be true.
Then followed a torrent of laughter and cheers:
Then the ominous words "It's a Boo-"
Then, silence. Some fancied they heard in the air
A weary and wandering sigh
Then sounded like "-jum!" but the others declare
It was only a breeze that went by.

They hunted till darkness came on, but they found
Not a button, or feather, or mark,
By which they could tell that they stood on the ground
Where the Baker had met with the Snark.

In the midst of the word he was trying to say,
In the midst of his laughter and glee,
He had softly and suddenly vanished away---
For the Snark was a Boojum, you see.

Antosha Chekhonte—
Anton Chekhov

Anton Chekhov, also known as "Antosha Chekhonte," was born on January 17, 1860 in Taganrog, Russia. His early published works were mostly short comic sketches for humorous journals in the area. Chekhov's early work was done primarily to pay for his tuition and to support his immediate family, which had been bankrupted by his father's financial mismanagement and departure in 1876. Chekhov published these vignettes mostly under the pseudonym "Antosha Chekhonte" and became famous throughout Russia as a satirist, gradually working his way towards better-paying positions in St. Petersburg. As the years went on, he turned towards a more serious style of writing, publishing numerous short stories, novellas, and plays. He helped bring early modernism into theatre, and is now considered a pioneer of the movement. Chekhov was also a credible doctor and medical administrator throughout his life. He died from tuberculosis on July 14, 1905.

Vanka"

Nine-year-old Vanka Zhukov, who had been apprentice to the shoe-maker Aliakhin for three months, did not go to bed the night before Christmas. He waited till the master and mistress and the assistants had gone out to an early church-service, to procure from his employer's cupboard a small phial of ink and a penholder with a rusty nib; then, spreading a crumpled sheet of paper in front of him, he began to write.

Before, however, deciding to make the first letter, he looked furtively at the door and at the window, glanced several times at the sombre ikon, on either side of which stretched shelves full of lasts, and heaved a heart-rending sigh. The sheet of paper was spread on a bench, and he himself was on his knees in front of it.

"Dear Grandfather Konstantin Makarych," he wrote, "I am writing you a letter. I wish you a Happy Christmas and all God's holy best. I have no mamma or papa, you are all I have."

Vanka gave a look towards the window in which shone the reflection of his candle, and vividly pictured to himself his grandfather, Konstantin Makarych, who was night-watchman at Messrs. Zhivarev. He was a small, lean, unusually lively and active old man of sixty-five, always smiling and blear-eyed. All day he slept in the servants' kitchen or trifled with the cooks. At night, enveloped in an ample sheep-skin coat, he strayed round the domain tapping with his cudgel. Behind him, each hanging its head, walked the old bitch Kashtanka, and the dog Viun, so named because of his black coat and long body and his resemblance to a loach. Viun was an unusually civil and friendly dog, looking as kindly at a stranger as at his masters, but he was not to be trusted. Beneath his deference and humbleness was hid the most inquisitorial maliciousness. No one knew better than he how to sneak up and take a bite at a leg, or slip into the larder or steal a muzhik's chicken. More than once they had nearly broken his hind-legs, twice he had been hung up, every week he was nearly flogged to death, but he always recovered.

At this moment, for certain, Vanka's grandfather must be standing at the gate, blinking his eyes at the bright red windows of the village church, stamping his feet in their high-felt boots, and jesting with the people in the yard; his cudgel will be hanging from his belt, he will be hugging himself with cold, giving a little dry, old man's cough, and at times pinching a servant-girl or a cook.

"Won't we take some snuff?" he asks, holding out his snuff-box to the women. The women take a pinch of snuff, and sneeze.

The old man goes into indescribable ecstasies, breaks into loud laughter, and cries:

"Off with it, it will freeze to your nose!"

He gives his snuff to the dogs, too. Kashtanka sneezes, twitches her nose, and walks away offended. Viun deferentially refuses to sniff and wags his tail. It is glorious weather, not a breath of wind, clear, and frosty; it is a dark night, but the whole village, its white roofs and streaks of smoke from the chimneys, the trees silvered with hoar-frost, and the snowdrifts, you can see it all. The sky scintillates with bright twinkling stars, and the Milky Way stands out so clearly that it looks as if it had been polished and rubbed over with snow for the holidays...

Vanka sighs, dips his pen in the ink, and continues to write:

"Last night I got a thrashing, my master dragged me by my hair into the yard, and belaboured me with a shoe-maker's stirrup, because, while I was rocking his brat in its cradle, I unfortunately fell asleep. And during the week, my mistress told me to clean a herring, and I began by its tail, so she took the herring and stuck its snout into my face. The assistants tease me, send me to the tavern for vodka, make me steal the master's cucumbers, and the master beats me with whatever is handy. Food there is none; in the morning it's bread, at dinner gruel, and in the evening bread again. As for tea or sour-cabbage soup, the master and the mistress themselves guzzle that. They make me sleep in the vestibule, and when their brat cries, I don't sleep at all, but have to rock the cradle. Dear Grandpapa, for Heaven's sake, take me away from here, home to our village, I can't bear this any more... I bow to the ground to you, and will pray to God for ever and ever, take me from here or I shall die..."

The corners of Vanka's mouth went down, he rubbed his eyes with his dirty fist, and sobbed.

"I'll grate your tobacco for you," he continued, "I'll pray to God for you, and if there is anything wrong, then flog me like the grey goat. And if you really think I shan't find work, then I'll ask the manager, for Christ's sake, to let me clean the boots, or I'll go instead of Fedya as underherdsman. Dear Grandpapa, I can't bear this any more, it'll kill me... I wanted to run away to our village, but I have no boots, and I was afraid of the frost, and when I grow up I'll look after you, no one shall harm you, and when you die I'll pray for the repose of your soul, just like I do for mamma Pelagueya.

"As for Moscow, it is a large town, there are all gentlemen's houses, lots of horses, no sheep, and the dogs are not vicious. The children don't come round at Christmas with a star, no one is allowed to sing in the choir, and once I saw in a shop window hooks on a line and fishing rods, all for sale, and for every kind of fish, awfully convenient. And there was one hook which would catch a sheat-fish weighing a pound. And there are shops with guns, like the master's, and I am sure they must cost 100 rubles each. And in the meat-shops there are woodcocks, partridges, and hares, but who shot them or where they come from, the shopman won't say.

"Dear Grandpapa, and when the masters give a Christmas tree, take a golden walnut and hide it in my green box. Ask the young lady, Olga Ignatyevna, for it, say it's for Vanka."

Vanka sighed convulsively, and again stared at the window. He remembered that his grandfather always went to the forest for the Christmas tree, and took his grandson with him. What happy times! The frost crackled, his grandfather crackled, and as they both did, Vanka did the same. Then before cutting down the Christmas tree his grandfather smoked his pipe, took a long pinch of snuff, and made fun of poor frozen little Vanka... The young fir trees, wrapt in hoar-frost, stood motionless, waiting for which of them would die. Suddenly a hare springing from somewhere would dart over the snowdrift... His grandfather could not help shouting:

"Catch it, catch it, catch it! Ah, short-tailed devil!"

When the tree was down, his grandfather dragged it to the master's house, and there they set about decorating it. The young lady, Olga Ignatyevna, Vanka's great friend, busied herself most about it. When little Vanka's mother, Pelagueya, was still alive, and was servant-woman in the house, Olga Ignatyevna used to stuff him with sugar-candy, and, having nothing to do, taught him to read, write, count up to one hundred, and even to dance the quadrille. When Pelagueya died, they placed the orphan Vanka in the kitchen with his grandfather, and from the kitchen he was sent to Moscow to Aliakhin, the shoemaker.

"Come quick, dear Grandpapa," continued Vanka, "I beseech you for Christ's sake take me from here. Have pity on a poor orphan, for here they beat me, and I am frightfully hungry, and so sad that I can't tell you, I cry all the time. The other day the master hit me on the head with a last; I fell to the ground, and only just returned to life. My life is a misfortune, worse than any dog's... I send greetings to Aliona, to one-eyed Tegor, and the coachman, and don't let any one have my mouth-organ. I remain, your grandson, Ivan Zhukov, dear Grandpapa, do come."

Vanka folded his sheet of paper in four, and put it into an envelope purchased the night before for a kopek. He thought a little, dipped the pen into the ink, and wrote the address:

"The village, to my grandfather." He then scratched his head, thought again, and added: "Konstantin Makarych." Pleased at not having been interfered with in his writing, he put on his cap, and, without putting on his sheep-skin coat, ran out in his shirt-sleeves into the street.

The shopman at the poulterer's, from whom he had inquired the night before, had told him that letters were to be put into post-boxes, and from there they were conveyed over the whole earth in mail troikas by drunken post-boys and to the sound of bells. Vanka ran to the first post-box and slipped his precious letter into the slit.

An hour afterwards, lulled by hope, he was sleeping soundly. In his dreams he saw a stove, by the stove his grandfather sitting with his legs dangling down, barefooted, and reading a letter to the cooks, and Viun walking round the stove wagging his tail.

O. Henry—William Sydney Porter

William Sidney Porter, best known by his pseudonym "O. Henry," was born on September 11th, 1862 in Greensboro, North Carolina. Porter read constantly throughout his youth, but did not seriously pursue writing until his mid-twenties. Throughout his different careers, Porter contributed short stories and sketches to various publications in Texas, where he resided. In 1896, he was indicted and eventually charged for embezzling funds from the First National Bank of Austin. While serving a three year sentence, Porter continued to write short stories under an assortment of pseudonyms, but became well-known for his stories written under the name of "O. Henry," beginning in 1899. Porter produced hundreds of short stories throughout his life, and is known for his twist endings, witt, and wry humor, as well as his ability to capture different elements of society. He died on June 5th, 1910 in New York City, New York.

A Midsummer Knight's Dream

"The knights are dead;
Their swords are rust.
Except a few who have to hust-
Le all the time
To raise the dust."

Dear Reader: It was summertime. The sun glared down upon the city with pitiless ferocity. It is difficult for the sun to be ferocious and exhibit compunction simultaneously. The heat was—oh, bother thermometers!—who cares for standard measures, anyhow? It was so hot that—

The roof gardens put on so many extra waiters that you could hope to get your gin fizz now—as soon as all the other people got theirs. The hospitals were putting in extra cots for bystanders. For when little, woolly dogs loll their tongues out and say "woof, woof!" at the fleas that bite 'em, and nervous old black bombazine ladies screech "Mad dog!" and policemen begin to shoot, somebody is going to get hurt. The man from Pompton, N.J., who always wears an overcoat in July, had turned up in a Broadway hotel drinking hot Scotches and enjoying his annual ray from the calcium. Philanthropists were petitioning the Legislature to pass a bill requiring builders to make tenement fire-escapes more commodious, so that families might die all together of the heat instead of one or two at a time. So many men were telling you about the number of baths they took each day that you wondered how they got along after the real lessee of the apartment came back to town and thanked 'em for taking such good care of it. The young man who called loudly for cold beef and beer in the restaurant, protesting that roast pullet and Burgundy was really too heavy for such weather, blushed when he met your eye, for you had heard him all winter calling, in modest tones, for the same ascetic viands. Soup, pocketbooks, shirt waists, actors and baseball excuses grew thinner. Yes, it was summertime.

A man stood at Thirty-fourth street waiting for a downtown car. A man of forty, gray-haired, pink-faced, keen, nervous, plainly dressed, with a harassed look around the eyes. He wiped his forehead and laughed loudly when a fat man with an outing look stopped and spoke with him.

"No, siree," he shouted with defiance and scorn. "None of your old mosquito-haunted swamps and skyscraper mountains without elevators for me. When I want to get away from hot weather I know how to do it. New York, sir, is the finest summer resort in the country. Keep in the shade and watch your diet, and don't get too far away from an electric fan. Talk about your Adirondacks and your Catskills! There's more solid comfort in the borough of Manhattan than in all the rest of the country together. No, siree! No tramping up perpendicular cliffs and being waked up at 4 in the morning by a million flies, and eating canned goods straight from the city for me. Little old New York will take a few select summer boarders; comforts and conveniences of homes—that's the ad. that I answer every time."

"You need a vacation," said the fat man, looking closely at the other. "You haven't been away from town in years. Better come with me for two weeks, anyhow. The trout in the Beaverkill are jumping at anything now that looks like a fly. Harding writes me that he landed a three-pound brown last week."

"Nonsense!" cried the other man. "Go ahead, if you like, and boggle around in rubber boots wearing yourself out trying to catch fish. When I want one I go to a cool restaurant and order it. I laugh at you fellows whenever I think of you hustling around in the heat in the country thinking you are having a good time. For me Father Knickerbocker's little improved farm with the big shady lane running through the middle of it."

The fat man sighed over his friend and went his way. The man who thought New York was the greatest summer resort in the country boarded a car and went buzzing down to his office. On the way he threw away his newspaper and looked up at a ragged patch of sky above the housetops.

"Three pounds!" he muttered, absently. "And Harding isn't a liar. I believe, if I could—but it's impossible—they've got to have another month—another month at least."

In his office the upholder of urban midsummer joys dived, headforemost, into the swimming pool of business. Adkins, his clerk, came and added a spray of letters, memoranda and telegrams.

At 5 o'clock in the afternoon the busy man leaned back in his office chair, put his feet on the desk and mused aloud:

"I wonder what kind of bait Harding used."

She was all in white that day; and thereby Compton lost a bet to Gaines. Compton had wagered she would wear light blue, for she knew that was his favorite color, and Compton was a millionaire's son, and that almost laid him open to the charge of betting on a sure thing. But white was her choice, and Gaines held up his head with twenty-five's lordly air.

The little summer hotel in the mountains had a lively crowd that year. There were two or three young college men and a couple of artists and a young naval officer on one side. On the other there were enough beauties among the young ladies for the correspondent of a society paper to refer to them as a "bevy." But the moon among the stars was Mary Sewell. Each one of the young men greatly desired to arrange matters so that he could pay her millinery bills, and fix the furnace, and have her do away with the "Sewell" part of her name forever. Those who could stay only a week or two went away hinting at pistols and blighted hearts. But Compton stayed like the mountains themselves, for he could afford it. And Gaines stayed because he was a fighter and wasn't afraid of millionaire's sons, and—well, he adored the country.

"What do you think, Miss Mary?" he said once. "I knew a duffer in New York who claimed to like it in the summer time. Said you could keep cooler there than you could in the woods. Wasn't he an awful silly? I don't think I could breathe on Broadway after the 1st of June."

"Mamma was thinking of going back week after next," said Miss Mary with a lovely frown.

"But when you think of it," said Gaines, "there are lots of jolly places in town in the summer. The roof gardens, you know, and the—er—the roof gardens."

Deepest blue was the lake that day—the day when they had the mock tournament, and the men rode clumsy farm horses around in a glade in the woods and caught curtain rings on the end of a lance. Such fun!

Cool and dry as the finest wine came the breath of the shadowed forest. The valley below was a vision seen through an opal haze. A white mist from hidden falls blurred the green of a hand's breadth of tree tops half-way down the gorge. Youth made merry hand-in-hand with young summer. Nothing on Broadway like that.

The villagers gathered to see the city folks pursue their mad drollery. The woods rang with the laughter of pixies and naiads and sprites. Gaines caught most of the rings. His was the privilege to crown the queen of the tournament. He was the conquering knight—as far as the rings went. On his arm he wore a white scarf. Compton wore light blue. She had declared her preference for blue, but she wore white that day.

Gaines looked about for the queen to crown her. He heard her merry laugh, as if from the clouds. She had slipped away and climbed Chimney Rock, a little granite bluff, and stood there, a white fairy among the laurels, fifty feet above their heads.

Instantly he and Compton accepted the implied challenge. The bluff was easily mounted at the rear, but the front offered small hold to hand or foot. Each man quickly selected his route and began to climb, A crevice, a bush, a slight projection, a vine or tree branch—all of these were aids that counted in the race. It was all foolery—there was no stake; but there was youth in it, cross reader, and light hearts, and something else that Miss Clay writes so charmingly about.

Gaines gave a great tug at the root of a laurel and pulled himself to Miss Mary's feet. On his arm he carried the wreath of roses; and while the villagers and summer boarders screamed and applauded below he placed it on the queen's brow.

"You are a gallant knight," said Miss Mary.

"If I could be your true knight always," began Gaines, but Miss Mary laughed him dumb, for Compton scrambled over the edge of the rock one minute behind time.

What a twilight that was when they drove back to the hotel! The opal of the valley turned slowly to purple, the dark woods framed the lake as a mirror, the tonic air stirred the very soul in one. The first pale stars came out over the mountain tops where yet a faint glow of—

"I beg your pardon, Mr. Gaines," said Adkins.

The man who believed New York to be the finest summer resort in the world opened his eyes and kicked over the mucilage bottle on his desk.

"I—I believe I was asleep," he said.

38

"It's the heat," said Adkins. "It's something awful in the city these"—

"Nonsense!" said the other. "The city beats the country ten to one in summer. Fools go out tramping in muddy brooks and wear themselves out trying to catch little fish as long as your finger. Stay in town and keep comfortable—that's my idea."

"Some letters just came," said Adkins. "I thought you might like to glance at them before you go."

Let us look over his shoulder and read just a few lines of one of them:

My Dear, Dear Husband: Just received your letter ordering us to stay another month. ... Rita's cough is almost gone. ... Johnny has simply gone wild like a little Indian ... Will be the making of both children ... work so hard, and I know that your business can hardly afford to keep us here so long ... best man that ever ... you always pretend that you like the city in summer ... trout fishing that you used to be so fond of ... and all to keep us well and happy ... come to you if it were not doing the babies so much good. ... I stood last evening on Chimney Rock in exactly the same spot where I was when you put the wreath of roses on my head ... through all the world ... when you said you would be my true knight ... fifteen years ago, dear, just think! ... have always been that to me ... ever and ever,
Mary.

The man who said he thought New York the finest summer resort in the country dropped into a café on his way home and had a glass of beer under an electric fan.

"Wonder what kind of a fly old Harding used," he said to himself.

Eleanor Putnam——Harriet Bates

Harriet Bates, known best by her pseudonym "Eleanor Putnam," was born on July 30th, 1856 in Quincy, Illinois. Bates moved to Salem, Massachusetts in 1865, and wrote frequently throughout her childhood. She took on her grandmother's maiden name "Eleanor Putnam" as a pseudonym, and began to contribute to different American periodicals. In 1882, she married author Arlo Bates with whom she eventually published *Prince Vance*. In 1885, she started writing a number of sketches about society in Salem for the *Atlantic Monthly*, which were well-known for their characterization of everyday life in Salem, as well as for their wit. Arlo Bates eventually published Harriet Bates's sketches, along with a book, posthumously. Bates died in March of 1866 in Boston, Massachusetts.

Old Salem Shops

I WONDER how many people have memories as vivid as mine of the quaint shops which a score of years ago stood placidly along the quiet streets of Salem. In the Salem of to-day there are few innovations. Not many modern buildings have replaced the time-honored landmarks; yet twenty years ago Salem, in certain aspects, was far more like an old colonial town than it is now. When the proprietor of an old shop died it was seldom that a new master entered. Nobody new ever came to Salem, and everybody then living there had already his legitimate occupation. The old shops, lacking tenants, went to sleep. Their green shutters were closed, and they were laid up in ordinary without comment from any one.

I remember one shop of the variety known in Salem as "button stores." It was kept by two quaint old sisters, whose family name I never knew. We always called them Miss Martha and Miss Sibyl. Miss Martha was the older, and sported a magnificent turban of wonderful construction. Miss Sibyl wore caps and little wintry curls. Both had short-waisted gowns, much shirred toward the belts, and odd little housewives of green leather, which hung from their apron-bindings by green ribbons.

Their wares were few and faded. They had a sparse collection of crewels, old-fashioned laces, little crimped cakes of white wax, and emery balls in futile imitation of strawberries. They sold handkerchiefs, antiquated gauze, and brocaded ribbons, and did embroidery stamping for ladies with much care and deliberation. I remember being once sent to take to these ladies an article which was to be stamped with a single letter. Miss Martha consulted at some length with her sister, and then, with an air of gentle importance, said to me: "Tell your mother, dear, that sister Sibyl will have it ready in one week, certainly."

On another occasion Miss Sibyl had chanced to give me a penny too much in change; discovering which before I was well away, I returned to the shop and told her of the mistake. Miss Sibyl dropped the penny into the little till,—so slender were the means of these old gentlewomen that I believe even a penny was of importance to them,—and in her gentle voice she asked, "What is your name, dear?" and when I told her she replied, approvingly, "Well, you are an honest child, and you may go home and tell your mother that Miss Sibyl said so." To this commendation she added the gift of a bit of pink gauze ribbon, brocaded with little yellow and lavender leaves, and I returned to my family in a condition of such conscious virtue that I am convinced that I must have been quite insufferable for some days following.

The only article in which these ladies dealt which specially concerned us children was a sort of gay-colored beads, such as were used in making bags and reticules—that fine old bead embroidery which some people show nowadays as the work of their great-grandmothers. These beads were highly valued by Salem children, and were sold for a penny a thimbleful. They were measured out in a small mustard-spoon of yellow wood, and it took three ladlefuls to fill the thimble. I cannot forget the air of placid and judicial gravity with which dear Miss Martha measured out a cent's worth of beads.

One winter day Miss Sibyl died. The green shutters of the shop were bowed with black ribbons, and a bit of rusty black crape fluttered from the knob of the half-glass door, inside of which the curtains were drawn as for a Sunday. For a whole week the shop was decorously closed. When it was reopened, only Miss Martha, a little older and grayer and more gently serious, stood behind the scantily filled show-case. My mother went in with me that day and bought some laces. Miss Martha folded each piece about a card and secured the ends with pins, after her usual careful fashion, and made out the quaint little receipted bill with which she always insisted on furnishing customers. As she handed the parcel across the counter she answered a look in my mother's eyes.

"I did not think she would go first," she said, simply. "Sibyl was very young to die."

In the following autumn came Miss Martha's turn to go. Then the shutters were closed forever. Nobody took the store. The winter snows drifted unchecked into the narrow doorway, and the bit of black crape affixed to the latch by friendly hands waved forlornly in the chilly winds and shivered in the air,—a thing to affect a child weirdly, and to be hastened past with a "creepy" sensation in the uncertain grayness of a winter twilight.

Mark Twain—Samuel Clemens

       Samuel Clemens, best known as "Mark Twain," was born on November 30, 1835. Twain was an American writer,   humorist, entrepreneur, publisher, and lecturer. After losing his dad at the age of 11, Clemens left school to become a printing apprentice and later became a typesetter where he contributed articles to the *Hannibal Journal.* At the age of 18, he worked as a printer in New York City, Philadelphia, St. Louis, and then Cincinnati. As Clemens grew older, he began to travel and experience more as a writer. He was a steamboat pilot at the age of 21 and derived his pen name, "Mark Twain," from terminology used by river boatmen to signify the depth of water. Slavery became a big theme in his work while it was legal in Missouri, and heavily influenced the second of his two most famous works, *The Adventures of Huckleberry Finn*, published in 1885. He died on April 21, 1910 in Redding, Connecticut.

A Dog's Tale

CHAPTER I

My father was a St. Bernard, my mother was a collie, but I am a Presbyterian. This is what my mother told me, I do not know these nice distinctions myself. To me they are only fine large words meaning nothing. My mother had a fondness for such; she liked to say them, and see other dogs look surprised and envious, as wondering how she got so much education. But, indeed, it was not real education; it was only show: she got the words by listening in the dining-room and drawing-room when there was company, and by going with the children to Sunday-school and listening there; and whenever she heard a large word she said it over to herself many times, and so was able to keep it until there was a dogmatic gathering in the neighborhood, then she would get it off, and surprise and distress them all, from pocket-pup to mastiff, which rewarded her for all her trouble. If there was a stranger he was nearly sure to be suspicious, and when he got his breath again he would ask her what it meant. And she always told him. He was never expecting this but thought he would catch her; so when she told him, he was the one that looked ashamed, whereas he had thought it was going to be she. The others were always waiting for this, and glad of it and proud of her, for they knew what was going to happen, because they had had experience. When she told the meaning of a big word they were all so taken up with admiration that it never occurred to any dog to doubt if it was the right one; and that was natural, because, for one thing, she answered up so promptly that it seemed like a dictionary speaking, and for another thing, where could they find out whether it was right or not? for she was the only cultivated dog there was. By and by, when I was older, she brought home the word Unintellectual, one time, and worked it pretty hard all the week at different gatherings, making much unhappiness and despondency; and it was at this time that I noticed that during that week she was asked for the meaning at eight different assemblages, and flashed out a fresh definition every time, which showed me that she had more presence of mind than culture, though I said nothing, of course. She had one word which she always kept on hand, and ready, like a life-preserver, a kind of emergency word to strap on when she was likely to get washed overboard in a sudden way—that was the word Synonymous. When she happened to fetch out a long word which had had its day weeks before and its prepared meanings gone to her dump-pile, if there was a stranger there of course it knocked him groggy for a couple of minutes, then he would come to, and by that time she would be away down wind on another tack, and not expecting anything; so when he'd hail and ask her to cash in, I (the only dog on the inside of her game) could see her canvas flicker a moment—but only just a moment—then it would belly out taut and full, and she would say, as calm as a summer's day, "It's synonymous with supererogation," or some godless long reptile of a word like that, and go placidly about and skim away on the next tack, perfectly comfortable, you know, and leave that stranger looking profane and embarrassed, and the initiated slatting the floor with their tails in unison and their faces transfigured with a holy joy.

And it was the same with phrases. She would drag home a whole phrase, if it had a grand sound, and play it six nights and two matinees, and explain it a new way every time—which she had to, for all she cared for was the phrase; she wasn't interested in what it meant, and knew those dogs hadn't wit enough to catch her, anyway. Yes, she was a daisy! She got so she wasn't afraid of anything, she had such confidence in the ignorance of those creatures. She even brought anecdotes that she had heard the family and the dinner-guests laugh and shout over; and as a rule she got the nub of one chestnut hitched onto another chestnut, where, of course, it didn't fit and hadn't any point; and when she delivered the nub she fell over and rolled on the floor and laughed and barked in the most insane way, while I could see that she was wondering to herself why it didn't seem as funny as it did when she first heard it. But no harm was done; the others rolled and barked too, privately ashamed of themselves for not seeing the point, and never suspecting that the fault was not with them and there wasn't any to see.

You can see by these things that she was of a rather vain and frivolous character; still, she had virtues, and enough to make up, I think. She had a kind heart and gentle ways, and never harbored resentments for injuries done her, but put them easily out of her mind and forgot them; and she taught her children her kindly way, and from her we learned also to be brave and prompt in time of danger, and not to run away, but face the peril that threatened friend or stranger, and help him the best we could without stopping to think what the cost might be to us. And she taught us not by words only, but by example, and that is the best way and the surest and the most lasting. Why, the brave things she did, the splendid things! she was just a soldier; and so modest about it—well, you couldn't help admiring her, and you couldn't help imitating her; not even a King Charles spaniel could remain entirely despicable in her society. So, as you see, there was more to her than her education.

CHAPTER II

When I was well grown, at last, I was sold and taken away, and I never saw her again. She was broken-hearted, and so was I, and we cried; but she comforted me as well as she could, and said we were sent into this world for a wise and good purpose, and must do our duties without repining, take our life as we might find it, live it for the best good of others, and never mind about the results; they were not our affair. She said men who did like this would have a noble and beautiful reward by and by in another world, and although we animals would not go there, to do well and right without reward would give to our brief lives a worthiness and dignity which in itself would be a reward. She had gathered these things from time to time when she had gone to the Sunday-school with the children, and had laid them up in her memory more carefully than she had done with those other words and phrases; and she had studied them deeply, for her good and ours. One may see by this that she had a wise and thoughtful head, for all there was so much lightness and vanity in it.

So we said our farewells, and looked our last upon each other through our tears; and the last thing she said—keeping it for the last to make me remember it the better, I think—was, "In memory of me, when there is a time of danger to another do not think of yourself, think of your mother, and do as she would do."

Do you think I could forget that? No.

CHAPTER III

It was such a charming home!—my new one; a fine great house, with pictures, and delicate decorations, and rich furniture, and no gloom anywhere, but all the wilderness of dainty colors lit up with flooding sunshine; and the spacious grounds around it, and the great garden—oh, greensward, and noble trees, and flowers, no end! And I was the same as a member of the family; and they loved me, and petted me, and did not give me a new name, but called me by my old one that was dear to me because my mother had given it me—Aileen Mavourneen. She got it out of a song; and the Grays knew that song, and said it was a beautiful name.

Mrs. Gray was thirty, and so sweet and so lovely, you cannot imagine it; and Sadie was ten, and just like her mother, just a darling slender little copy of her, with auburn tails down her back, and short frocks; and the baby was a year old, and plump and dimpled, and fond of me, and never could get enough of hauling on my tail, and hugging me, and laughing out its innocent happiness; and Mr. Gray was thirty-eight, and tall and slender and handsome, a little bald in front, alert, quick in his movements, business-like, prompt, decided, unsentimental, and with that kind of trim-chiseled face that just seems to glint and sparkle with frosty intellectuality! He was a renowned scientist. I do not know what the word means, but my mother would know how to use it and get effects. She would know how to depress a rat-terrier with it and make a lap-dog look sorry he came. But that is not the best one; the best one was Laboratory. My mother could organize a Trust on that one that would skin the tax-collars off the whole herd. The laboratory was not a book, or a picture, or a place to wash your hands in, as the college president's dog said—no, that is the lavatory; the laboratory is quite different, and is filled with jars, and bottles, and electrics, and wires, and strange machines; and every week other scientists came there and sat in the place, and used the machines, and discussed, and made what they called experiments and discoveries; and often I came, too, and stood around and listened, and tried to learn, for the sake of my mother, and in loving memory of her, although it was a pain to me, as realizing what she was losing out of her life and I gaining nothing at all; for try as I might, I was never able to make anything out of it at all.

Other times I lay on the floor in the mistress's work-room and slept, she gently using me for a foot-stool, knowing it pleased me, for it was a caress; other times I spent an hour in the nursery, and got well tousled and made happy; other times I watched by the crib there, when the baby was asleep and the nurse out for a few minutes on the baby's affairs; other times I romped and raced through the grounds and the garden with Sadie till we were tired out, then slumbered on the grass in the shade of a tree while she read her book; other times I went visiting among the neighbor dogs—for there were some most pleasant ones not far away, and one very handsome and courteous and graceful one, a curly-haired Irish setter by the name of Robin Adair, who was a Presbyterian like me, and belonged to the Scotch minister.

The servants in our house were all kind to me and were fond of me, and so, as you see, mine was a pleasant life. There could not be a happier dog that I was, nor a gratefuller one. I will say this for myself, for it is only the truth: I tried in all ways to do well and right, and honor my mother's memory and her teachings, and earn the happiness that had come to me, as best I could.

By and by came my little puppy, and then my cup was full, my happiness was perfect. It was the dearest little waddling thing, and so smooth and soft and velvety, and had such cunning little awkward paws, and such affectionate eyes, and such a sweet and innocent face; and it made me so proud to see how the children and their mother adored it, and fondled it, and exclaimed over every little wonderful thing it did. It did seem to me that life was just too lovely to—

Then came the winter. One day I was standing a watch in the nursery. That is to say, I was asleep on the bed. The baby was asleep in the crib, which was alongside the bed, on the side next the fireplace. It was the kind of crib that has a lofty tent over it made of gauzy stuff that you can see through. The nurse was out, and we two sleepers were alone. A spark from the wood-fire was shot out, and it lit on the slope of the tent. I suppose a quiet interval followed, then a scream from the baby awoke me, and there was that tent flaming up toward the ceiling! Before I could think, I sprang to the floor in my fright, and in a second was half-way to the door; but in the next half-second my mother's farewell

47

was sounding in my ears, and I was back on the bed again. I reached my head through the flames and dragged the baby out by the waist-band, and tugged it along, and we fell to the floor together in a cloud of smoke; I snatched a new hold, and dragged the screaming little creature along and out at the door and around the bend of the hall, and was still tugging away, all excited and happy and proud, when the master's voice shouted:

"Begone you cursed beast!" and I jumped to save myself; but he was furiously quick, and chased me up, striking furiously at me with his cane, I dodging this way and that, in terror, and at last a strong blow fell upon my left foreleg, which made me shriek and fall, for the moment, helpless; the cane went up for another blow, but never descended, for the nurse's voice rang wildly out, "The nursery's on fire!" and the master rushed away in that direction, and my other bones were saved.

The pain was cruel, but, no matter, I must not lose any time; he might come back at any moment; so I limped on three legs to the other end of the hall, where there was a dark little stairway leading up into a garret where old boxes and such things were kept, as I had heard say, and where people seldom went. I managed to climb up there, then I searched my way through the dark among the piles of things, and hid in the secretest place I could find. It was foolish to be afraid there, yet still I was; so afraid that I held in and hardly even whimpered, though it would have been such a comfort to whimper, because that eases the pain, you know. But I could lick my leg, and that did some good.

For half an hour there was a commotion downstairs, and shoutings, and rushing footsteps, and then there was quiet again. Quiet for some minutes, and that was grateful to my spirit, for then my fears began to go down; and fears are worse than pains—oh, much worse. Then came a sound that froze me. They were calling me—calling me by name—hunting for me!

It was muffled by distance, but that could not take the terror out of it, and it was the most dreadful sound to me that I had ever heard. It went all about, everywhere, down there: along the halls, through all the rooms, in both stories, and in the basement and the cellar; then outside, and farther and farther away—then back, and all about the house again, and I thought it would never, never stop. But at last it did, hours and hours after the vague twilight of the garret had long ago been blotted out by black darkness.

Then in that blessed stillness my terrors fell little by little away, and I was at peace and slept. It was a good rest I had, but I woke before the twilight had come again. I was feeling fairly comfortable, and I could think out a plan now. I made a very good one; which was, to creep down, all the way down the back stairs, and hide behind the cellar door, and slip out and escape when the iceman came at dawn, while he was inside filling the refrigerator; then I would hide all day, and start on my journey when night came; my journey to—well, anywhere where they would not know me and betray me to the master. I was feeling almost cheerful now; then suddenly I thought: Why, what would life be without my puppy!

That was despair. There was no plan for me; I saw that; I must stay where I was; stay, and wait, and take what might come—it was not my affair; that was what life is—my mother had said it. Then—well, then the calling began again! All my sorrows came back. I said to myself, the master will never forgive. I did not know what I had done to make him so bitter and so unforgiving, yet I judged it was something a dog could not understand, but which was clear to a man and dreadful.

They called and called—days and nights, it seemed to me. So long that the hunger and thirst near drove me mad, and I recognized that I was getting very weak. When you are this way you sleep a great deal, and I did. Once I woke in an awful fright—it seemed to me that the calling was right there in the garret! And so it was: it was Sadie's voice, and she was crying; my name was falling from her lips all broken, poor thing, and I could not believe my ears for the joy of it when I heard her say:

"Come back to us—oh, come back to us, and forgive—it is all so sad without our—"

I broke in with SUCH a grateful little yelp, and the next moment Sadie was plunging and stumbling through the darkness and the lumber and shouting for the family to hear, "She's found, she's found!"

The days that followed—well, they were wonderful. The mother and Sadie and the servants—why, they just seemed to worship me. They couldn't seem to make me a bed that was fine enough; and as for food, they couldn't be satisfied with anything but game and delicacies that were out of season; and every day the friends and neighbors flocked in to hear about my heroism—that was the name they called it by, and it means agriculture. I remember my mother pulling it on a kennel once, and explaining it in that way, but didn't say what agriculture was, except that it was synonymous with intramural incandescence; and a dozen times a day Mrs. Gray and Sadie would tell the tale to new-comers, and say I risked my life to save the baby's, and both of us had burns to prove it, and then the company would pass me around and pet me and exclaim about me, and you could see the pride in the eyes of Sadie and her mother; and when the people wanted to know what made me limp, they looked ashamed and changed the subject, and sometimes when people hunted them this way and that way with questions about it, it looked to me as if they were going to cry.

And this was not all the glory; no, the master's friends came, a whole twenty of the most distinguished people, and had me in the laboratory, and discussed me as if I was a kind of discovery; and some of them said it was wonderful in a dumb beast, the finest exhibition of instinct they could call to mind; but the master said, with vehemence, "It's far above instinct; it's REASON, and many a man, privileged to be saved and go with you and me to a better world by right of its possession, has less of it that this poor silly quadruped that's foreordained to perish;" and then he laughed, and said: "Why, look at me—I'm a sarcasm! bless you, with all my grand intelligence, the only thing I inferred was that the dog had gone mad and was destroying the child, whereas but for the beast's intelligence—it's REASON, I tell you!—the child would have perished!"

They disputed and disputed, and I was the very center of subject of it all, and I wished my mother could know that this grand honor had come to me; it would have made her proud.

Then they discussed optics, as they called it, and whether a certain injury to the brain would produce blindness or not, but they could not agree about it, and said they must test it by experiment by and by; and next they discussed plants, and that interested me, because in the summer Sadie and I had planted seeds—I helped her dig the holes, you know—and after days and days a little shrub or a flower came up there, and it was a wonder how that could happen; but it did, and I wished I could talk—I would have told those people about it and shown then how much I knew, and been all alive with the subject; but I didn't care for the optics; it was dull, and when they came back to it again it bored me, and I went to sleep.

Pretty soon it was spring, and sunny and pleasant and lovely, and the sweet mother and the children patted me and the puppy good-by, and went away on a journey and a visit to their kin, and the master wasn't any company for us, but we played together and had good times, and the servants were kind and friendly, so we got along quite happily and counted the days and waited for the family.

And one day those men came again, and said, now for the test, and they took the puppy to the laboratory, and I limped three-leggedly along, too, feeling proud, for any attention shown to the puppy was a pleasure to me, of course. They discussed and experimented, and then suddenly the puppy shrieked, and they set him on the floor, and he went staggering around, with his head all bloody, and the master clapped his hands and shouted:

"There, I've won—confess it! He's as blind as a bat!"

And they all said:

"It's so—you've proved your theory, and suffering humanity owes you

50

a great debt from henceforth," and they crowded around him, and wrung his hand cordially and thankfully, and praised him.

But I hardly saw or heard these things, for I ran at once to my little darling, and snuggled close to it where it lay, and licked the blood, and it put its head against mine, whimpering softly, and I knew in my heart it was a comfort to it in its pain and trouble to feel its mother's touch, though it could not see me. Then it dropped down, presently, and its little velvet nose rested upon the floor, and it was still, and did not move any more.

Soon the master stopped discussing a moment, and rang in the footman, and said, "Bury it in the far corner of the garden," and then went on with the discussion, and I trotted after the footman, very happy and grateful, for I knew the puppy was out of its pain now, because it was asleep. We went far down the garden to the farthest end, where the children and the nurse and the puppy and I used to play in the summer in the shade of a great elm, and there the footman dug a hole, and I saw he was going to plant the puppy, and I was glad, because it would grow and come up a fine handsome dog, like Robin Adair, and be a beautiful surprise for the family when they came home; so I tried to help him dig, but my lame leg was no good, being stiff, you know, and you have to have two, or it is no use. When the footman had finished and covered little Robin up, he patted my head, and there were tears in his eyes, and he said: "Poor little doggie, you saved HIS child!"

I have watched two whole weeks, and he doesn't come up! This last week a fright has been stealing upon me. I think there is something terrible about this. I do not know what it is, but the fear makes me sick, and I cannot eat, though the servants bring me the best of food; and they pet me so, and even come in the night, and cry, and say, "Poor doggie—do give it up and come home; don't break our hearts!" and all this terrifies me the more, and makes me sure something has happened. And I am so weak; since yesterday I cannot stand on my feet anymore. And within this hour the servants, looking toward the sun where it was sinking out of sight and the night chill coming on, said things I could not understand, but they carried something cold to my heart.

"Those poor creatures! They do not suspect. They will come home in the morning, and eagerly ask for the little doggie that did the brave deed, and who of us will be strong enough to say the truth to them: 'The humble little friend is gone where go the beasts that perish.'"

Voltaire——François-Marie Arouet

François Marie Arouet, best known by his pseudonym "Voltaire," was born on November 21st, 1694 in Paris, France. Arouet ran into frequent legal troubles for his criticism of the French government and its practices during his early literary career. Upon his release from an 11-month sentence in the Bastille in 1718, Arouet officially adopted the pseudonym "Voltaire." He found commercial and critical success that same year with his landmark play, *Oedipus*. In 1726, the French government exiled Arouet who immigrated to England. During his three year exile, he delved further into critical thought and theory. Throughout his life, Arouet was a proponent of freedom of speech and the separation of church and state, stances which frequently led to his works being banned. In 1759, Arouet published his magnum opus, *Candide*, and continued to write throughout the remainder of his life. He died in Paris France on May 30, 1778.

1.

The Good Brahmin
Does Happiness Result From Igno-
rance or From Knowledge?

In my travels I once happened to meet with an aged Brahmin. This man had a great share of understanding and prudence, and was very learned. He was also very rich, and his riches added greatly to his popularity, for, wanting nothing that wealth could procure, he had no desire to defraud any one. His family was admirably managed by three handsome wives, who always studied to please him, and when he was weary of their society, he had recourse to the study of philosophy.

Not far from his house, which was handsome, well furnished, and embellished with delightful gardens, dwelt an old Indian woman who was a great bigot, ignorant, and withal very poor.

"I wish," said the Brahmin to me one day, "I had never been born."

"Why so?" said I.

"Because," said he, "I have been studying these forty years, and I find it has been so much time lost. While I teach others I know nothing myself. The sense of my condition is so humiliating, it makes all things so distasteful to me, that life has become a burden. I have been born, and I exist in time, without knowing what time is. I am placed, as our wise men say, in the confines between two eternities, and yet I have no idea of eternity. I am composed of matter, I think, but have never been able to satisfy myself what it is that produces thought. I even am ignorant whether my understanding is a simple faculty I possess, like that of walking and digesting, or if I think with my head in the same manner as I take hold of a thing with my hands. I am not only thus in the dark with relation to the principles of thought, but the principles of my motions are entirely unknown to me. I do not know why I exist, and yet I am applied to every day for a solution of the enigma. I must return an answer, but can say nothing satisfactory on the subject. I talk a great deal, and when I have done speaking remain confounded and ashamed of what I have said.

"I am in still greater perplexity when I am asked if Brahma was produced by Vishnu, or if they have both existed from eternity. God is

53

my judge that I know nothing of the matter, as plainly appears by my answers. 'Reverend father,' says one, 'be pleased to inform me how evil is spread over the face of the earth.' I am as much at a loss as those who ask the question. Sometimes I tell them that everything is for the best; but those who have the gout or the stone—those who have lost their fortunes or their limbs in the wars—believe as little of this assertion as I do myself. I retire to my own house full of curiosity, and endeavor to enlighten my ignorance by consulting the writings of our ancient sages, but they only serve to bewilder me the more. When I talk with my brethren upon this subject, some tell me we ought to make the most of life and laugh at the world. Others think they know something, and lose themselves in vain and chimerical hypotheses. Every effort I make to solve the mystery adds to the load I feel. Sometimes I am ready to fall into despair when I reflect that, after all my researches, I neither know from whence I came, what I am, whither I shall go, or what is to become of me."

The condition in which I saw this good man gave me real concern. No one could be more rational, no one more open and honest. It appeared to me that the force of his understanding and the sensibility of his heart were the causes of his misery.

The same day I had a conversation with the old woman, his neighbor. I asked her if she had ever been unhappy for not understanding how her soul was made? She did not even comprehend my question. She had not, for the briefest moment in her life, had a thought about these subjects with which the good Brahmin had so tormented himself. She believed from the bottom of her heart in the metamorphoses of her god, Vishnu, and, provided she could get some of the sacred water of the Ganges in which to make her ablutions, she thought herself the happiest of women.

Struck with the happiness of this poor creature, I returned to my philosopher, whom I thus addressed:

"Are you not ashamed to be thus miserable when, not fifty yards from you, there is an old automaton who thinks of nothing and lives contented?"

"You are right," he replied. "I have said to myself a thousand times that I should be happy if I were but as ignorant as my old neighbor, and yet it is a happiness I do not desire."

This reply of the Brahmin made a greater impression on me than anything that had passed. I consulted my own heart and found that I myself should not wish to be happy on condition of being ignorant.

I submitted this matter to some philosophers, and they were all of my opinion; and yet, said I, there is something very contradictory in this manner of thinking, for, after all, what is the question? Is it not to be happy? What signifies it then whether we have understandings or whether we are fools? Besides, there is this to be said: those who are contented with their condition are sure of that content, while those who have the faculty of reasoning are not always sure of reasoning right. It is evident then, I continued, that we ought rather to wish not to have common sense, if that common sense contributes to our being either miserable or wicked.

They were all of my opinion, and yet not one of them could be found to accept of happiness on the terms of being ignorant. From hence I concluded that, although we may set a great value upon happiness, we set a still greater upon reason.

But after mature reflection upon this subject I still thought there was great madness in preferring reason to happiness. How is this contradiction to be explained? Like all other questions, a great deal may be said about it.

Section 2:
That's What (S)he Said

Acton Bell—Anne Brontë

Anne Brontë, otherwise known as "Acton Bell," was born on January 17, 1820 in Yorkshire, England. Anne began writing from an early age alongside her sisters, Charlotte and Emily. Before becoming a published author, Anne began working as a governess at the age of 19. She took on the pseudonym "Acton Bell" to publish a work of poetry with her sisters, *Poems by Currer, Ellis, and Acton Bell*, in 1846. Anne and her sisters wrote under pen names in order to have their work taken more seriously, although their initial collection garnered little success. She followed up her debut with *Agnes Grey*, published in 1847 and largely inspired by her time spent as a governess, and the *Tenant of Wildfell Hall*, published in 1848. Both novels were commercial successes and cemented Anne's status in the history of English literature. She died from tuberculosis on May 29th, 1849.

Stanzas

OH, weep not, love! each tear that springs
In those dear eyes of thine,
To me a keener suffering brings,
Than if they flowed from mine.
And do not droop! however drear
The fate awaiting thee;
For my sake combat pain and care,
And cherish life for me!

I do not fear thy love will fail;
Thy faith is true, I know;
But, oh, my love! thy strength is frail
For such a life of woe.

Were't not for this, I well could trace
(Though banished long from thee,)
Life's rugged path, and boldly face
The storms that threaten me.

Fear not for me–I've steeled my mind
Sorrow and strife to greet;
Joy with my love I leave behind,
Care with my friends I meet.

A mother's sad reproachful eye,
A father's scowling brow–
But he may frown and she may sigh:
I will not break my vow!
I love my mother, I revere
My sire, but fear not me–
Believe that Death alone can tear
This faithful heart from thee.

Currer Bell——Charlotte Brontë

Charlotte Brontë, otherwise known as "Currer Bell", was born on April 16th, 1816 in Yorkshire, England. Charlotte wrote frequently in her youth, creating a homemade magazine with her brother, Branwell, and developing an elaborate world to serve as the setting for their stories. Charlotte took on the pseudonym "Currer Bell" to publish a poetry anthology in 1846 along with her sisters, Anne and Emily, who also wrote under pen names. She kept the same pseudonym to publish her classic novel, *Jane Eyre*, one year later. *Jane Eyre* was immediately popular, and its success helped Anne and Emily Brontë secure publishing for their novels, *Agnes Grey* and *Wuthering Heights*, respectively. The passing of Branwell, Emily, and Anne in 1848 stunted Charlotte's work on her second novel, *Shirley*, which was eventually published in 1849. Despite her success during her own lifetime, Brontë is now remembered as a classic author who dealt with various themes which were deemed controversial at the time. Charlotte died during her pregnancy on March 31st, 1855.

Pilate's Wife's Dream

I've quenched my lamp, I struck it in that start
Which every limb convulsed, I heard it fall–
The crash blent with my sleep, I saw depart
Its light, even as I woke, on yonder wall;
Over against my bed, there shone a gleam
Strange, faint, and mingling also with my dream.
It sunk, and I am wrapt in utter gloom;
How far is night advanced, and when will day
Retinge the dusk and livid air with bloom,
And fill this void with warm, creative ray ?
Would I could sleep again till, clear and red,
Morning shall on the mountain-tops be spread!
I'd call my women, but to break their sleep,
Because my own is broken, were unjust;
They've wrought all day, and well-earned slumbers steep
Their labours in forgetfulness, I trust;
Let me my feverish watch with patience bear,
Thankful that none with me its sufferings share.
Yet, Oh, for light ! one ray would tranquilise
My nerves, my pulses, more than effort can;
I'll draw my curtain and consult the skies:
These trembling stars at dead of night look wan,
Wild, restless, strange, yet cannot be more drear
Than this my couch, shared by a nameless fear.
All black–one great cloud, drawn from east to west,
Conceals the heavens, but there are lights below;
Torches burn in Jerusalem, and cast
On yonder stony mount a lurid glow.
I see men stationed there, and gleaming spears;
A sound, too, from afar, invades my ears.
Dull, measured, strokes of axe and hammer ring
From street to street, not loud, but through the night
Distinctly heard–and some strange spectral thing
Is now upreared–and, fixed against the light
Of the pale lamps; defined upon that sky,
It stands up like a column, straight and high.
I see it all–I know the dusky sign–
A cross on Calvary, which Jews uprear
While Romans watch; and when the dawn shall shine
Pilate, to judge the victim will appear,
Pass sentence–yield him up to crucify;

And on that cross the spotless Christ must die.
Dreams, then, are true–for thus my vision ran;
    Surely some oracle has been with me,
The gods have chosen me to reveal their plan,
    To warn an unjust judge of destiny:
I, slumbering, heard and saw; awake I know,
Christ's coming death, and Pilate's life of woe.
    I do not weep for Pilate–who could prove
Regret for him whose cold and crushing sway
No prayer can soften, no appeal can move;
    Who tramples hearts as others trample clay,
    Yet with a faltering, an uncertain tread,
    That might stir up reprisal in the dead.
Forced to sit by his side and see his deeds;
Forced to behold that visage, hour by hour,
In whose gaunt lines, the abhorrent gazer reads
    A triple lust of gold, and blood, and power;
    A soul whom motives, fierce, yet abject, urge
Rome's servile slave, and Judah's tyrant scourge.
    How can I love, or mourn, or pity him ?
I, who so long my fettered hands have wrung;
I, who for grief have wept my eye-sight dim;
Because, while life for me was bright and young,
He robbed my youth–he quenched my life's fair ray–
He crushed my mind, and did my freedom slay.

    And at this hour–although I be his wife–
    He has no more of tenderness from me
    Than any other wretch of guilty life;
    Less, for I know his household privacy–
    I see him as he is–without a screen;
    And, by the gods, my soul abhors his mien !
Has he not sought my presence, dyed in blood–
Innocent, righteous blood, shed shamelessly ?
    And have I not his red salute withstood ?
    Aye,–when, as erst, he plunged all Galilee
    In dark bereavement–in affliction sore,
Mingling their very offerings with their gore.
    Then came he–in his eyes a serpent-smile,
    Upon his lips some false, endearing word,
And, through the streets of Salem, clanged the while,
    His slaughtering, hacking, sacrilegious sword–
    And I, to see a man cause men such woe,
    Trembled with ire–I did not fear to show.
And now, the envious Jewish priests have brought

Jesus–whom they in mockery call their king–
To have, by this grim power, their vengeance wrought;
By this mean reptile, innocence to sting.
Oh ! could I but the purposed doom avert,
And shield the blameless head from cruel hurt!
Accessible is Pilate's heart to fear,
Omens will shake his soul, like autumn leaf;
Could he this night's appalling vision hear,
This just man's bonds were loosed, his life were safe,
Unless that bitter priesthood should prevail,
And make even terror to their malice quail.
Yet if I tell the dream–but let me pause.
What dream ? Erewhile the characters were clear,
Graved on my brain–at once some unknown cause
Has dimmed and rased the thoughts, which now appear,
Like a vague remnant of some by-past scene;–
Not what will be, but what, long since, has been.
I suffered many things, I heard foretold
A dreadful doom for Pilate,–lingering woes,
In far, barbarian climes, where mountains cold
Built up a solitude of trackless snows,
There, he and grisly wolves prowled side by side,
There he lived famished–there methought he died;
But not of hunger, nor by malady;
I saw the snow around him, stained with gore;
I said I had no tears for such as he,
And, lo ! my cheek is wet–mine eyes run o'er;
I weep for mortal suffering, mortal guilt,
I weep the impious deed–the blood self-spilt.
More I recall not, yet the vision spread
Into a world remote, an age to come–
And still the illumined name of Jesus shed
A light, a clearness, through the enfolding gloom–
And still I saw that sign, which now I see,
That cross on yonder brow of Calvary.
What is this Hebrew Christ ? To me unknown,
His lineage–doctrine–mission–yet how clear,
Is God-like goodness, in his actions shewn !
How straight and stainless is his life's career !
The ray of Deity that rests on him,
In my eyes makes Olympian glory dim.
The world advances, Greek, or Roman rite
Suffices not the inquiring mind to stay;
The searching soul demands a purer light
To guide it on its upward, onward way;

Ashamed of sculptured gods–Religion turns
To where the unseen Jehovah's altar burns.
Our faith is rotten–all our rites defiled,
Our temples sullied, and methinks, this man,
With his new ordinance, so wise and mild,
Is come, even as he says, the chaff to fan
And sever from the wheat; but will his faith
Survive the terrors of to-morrow's death ?

* * * * *

I feel a firmer trust–a higher hope
Rise in my soul–it dawns with dawning day;
Lo ! on the Temple's roof–on Moriah's slope
Appears at length that clear, and crimson ray,
Which I so wished for when shut in by night;
Oh, opening skies, I hail, I bless your light !
Part, clouds and shadows ! glorious Sun appear !
Part, mental gloom ! Come insight from on high !
Dusk dawn in heaven still strives with daylight clear,
The longing soul, doth still uncertain sigh.
Oh ! to behold the truth–that sun divine,
How doth my bosom pant, my spirit pine !
This day, time travails with a mighty birth,
This day, Truth stoops from heaven and visits earth,
Ere night descends, I shall more surely know
What guide to follow, in what path to go;
I wait in hope–I wait in solemn fear,
The oracle of God–the sole–true God–to hear

Ellis Bell—Emily Jane Brontë

Emily Brontë, also known as "Ellis Bell," was born on July 30, 1818 in Yorkshire, England. The second youngest of the Brontë siblings, Emily grew up consuming the myriad of literary works present in her household. Her first published work came in 1846 with *Poems by Currer, Ellis, and Acton Bell*, an anthology of poems published with her sisters and the debut of Emily's pseudonym, "Ellis Bell." Emily only produced one other sizeable work, *Wuthering Heights*, published in 1847. The novel was heavily criticized on both construction and content when it first emerged, however, it now is looked upon with great literary esteem. Though all three Brontë sisters chose to publish under male names to be taken more seriously, Emily Brontë is known far more by her given name in contemporary literary thought. She was the first of the Brontë trio to die, succumbing to tuberculosis in December 19th, 1848.

Self-Interrogation

"THE evening passes fast away,
'Tis almost time to rest;
What thoughts has left the vanished day,
What feelings, in thy breast?
"The vanished day? It leaves a sense
Of labour hardly done;
Of little, gained with vast expense,–
A sense of grief alone!
"Time stands before the door of Death,
Upbraiding bitterly;
And Conscience, with exhaustless breath,
Pours black reproach on me:
"And though I've said that Conscience lies,
And Time should Fate condemn;
Still, sad Repentance clouds my eyes,
And makes me yield to them!
"Then art thou glad to seek repose?
Art glad to leave the sea,
And anchor all thy weary woes
In calm Eternity?
"Nothing regrets to see thee go–
Not one voice sobs ' farewell,'
And where thy heart has suffered so,
Canst thou desire to dwell?"
"Alas! The countless links are strong
That bind us to our clay;
The loving spirit lingers long,
And would not pass away!
"And rest is sweet, when laurelled fame
Will crown the soldier's crest;
But, a brave heart, with a tarnished name,
Would rather fight than rest."
"Well, thou hast fought for many a year,
Hast fought thy whole life through,
Hast humbled Falsehood, trampled Fear;
What is there left to do?"
"'Tis true, this arm has hotly striven,
Has dared what few would dare;
Much have I done, and freely given,
But little learnt to bear!"
"Look on the grave, where thou must sleep,

Thy last, and strongest foe;
It is endurance not to weep,
If that repose seem woe.
"The long war closing in defeat,
Defeat serenely borne,
Thy midnight rest may still be sweet,
And break in glorious morn!"

Silence Dogood—Benjamin Franklin

Benjamin Franklin, also known as "Silence Dogood," was born on January 17, 1706 in Boston, Massachusetts. Franklin took on the pseudonym at the age of sixteen, after constant frustration with not getting his work published in the *New England Courant*, a newspaper founded by his brother, James Franklin, and where Benjamin was an apprentice. This began a series of fourteen letters, first printed in 1722, that he wrote weekly and sent to his brother's print shop. The letters sparked curiosity and interest in readers, and gave him the recognition he sought for his work. James Franklin was upset when he found out the letters were written by his little brother, and Benjamin's writing for the paper, as well as his use of the pen name "Silence Dogood," ceased. Benjamin quit his apprenticeship and ran away to Philadelphia, and eventually London. He went on to become a prolific writer, scientist, theorist, and a Founding Father, publishing numerous influential works throughout his life. He died on April 17, 1790.

April 2, 1722 • Silence Dogood #1

To the Author of the *New-England Courant*.

Sir,

It may not be improper in the first place to inform your Readers, that I intend once a Fortnight to present them, by the Help of this Paper, with a short Epistle, which I presume will add somewhat to their Entertainment.

And since it is observed, that the Generality of People, now a days, are unwilling either to commend or dispraise what they read, until they are in some measure informed who or what the Author of it is, whether he be poor or rich, old or young, a Schollar or a Leather Apron Man, &c. and give their Opinion of the Performance, according to the Knowledge which they have of the Author's Circumstances, it may not be amiss to begin with a short Account of my past Life and present Condition, that the Reader may not be at a Loss to judge whether or no my Lucubrations are worth his reading.

At the time of my Birth, my Parents were on Ship-board in their Way from London to N. England. My Entrance into this troublesome World was attended with the Death of my Father, a Misfortune, which tho' I was not then capable of knowing, I shall never be able to forget; for as he, poor Man, stood upon the Deck rejoycing at my Birth, a merciless Wave entred the Ship, and in one Moment carry'd him beyond Reprieve. Thus, was the first Day which I saw, the last that was seen by my Father; and thus was my disconsolate Mother at once made both a Parent and a Widow.

When we arrived at Boston (which was not long after) I was put to Nurse in a Country Place, at a small Distance from the Town, where I went to School, and past my Infancy and Childhood in Vanity and Idleness, until I was bound out Apprentice, that I might no longer be a Charge to my Indigent Mother, who was put to hard Shifts for a Living.

My Master was a Country Minister, a pious good-natur'd young Man, and a Batchelor: he labour'd with all his Might to instil vertuous and godly Principles into my tender Soul, well knowing that it was the most suitable Time to make deep and lasting Impressions on the Mind, while it was yet untainted with Vice, free and unbiass'd. He endeavour'd that I might be instructed in all that Knowledge and Learning which is necessary for our Sex, and deny'd me no Accomplishment that could possibly be attained in a Country Place; such as all Sorts of Needle-Work, Writing, Arithmetick, &c. and observing that I took a more than ordinary Delight in reading ingenious Books, he gave me the free Use of his Library, which tho' it was but small, yet it was well chose, to inform the Understanding rightly, and enable the Mind to frame great and noble Ideas.

Before I had liv'd quite two Years with this Reverend Gentleman, my indulgent Mother departed this Life, leaving me as it were by my self, having no Relation on Earth within my Knowledge.

I will not abuse your Patience with a tedious Recital of all the frivolous Accidents of my Life, that happened from this Time until I arrived to Years of Discretion, only inform you that I liv'd a chearful Country Life, spending my leisure Time either in some innocent Diversion with the neighbouring Females, or in some shady Retirement, with the best of Company, Books. Thus I past away the Time with a Mixture of Profit and Pleasure, having no affliction but what was imaginary, and created in my own Fancy; as nothing is more common with us Women, than to be grieving for nothing, when we have nothing else to grieve for.

As I would not engross too much of your Paper at once, I will defer the Remainder of my Story until my next Letter; in the mean time desiring your Readers to exercise their Patience, and bear with my Humours now and then, because I shall trouble them but seldom. I am not insensible of the Impossibility of pleasing all, but I would not willingly displease any; and for those who will take Offence were none is intended, they are beneath the Notice of Your Humble Servant,

SILENCE DOGOOD.

George Eliot—Mary Ann Evans

Mary Anne Evans, and later Marian Evan, best known by the name of "George Eliot," was born on November 22, 1819 in Nuneaton, England. Evans' life was marred by various events that included the death of her mother and various tumultuous relationships. Evans spent much of her early years reading and writing, and she eventually chose the pen name "George Eliot" in order to publish her works to protect her reputation while trying new approaches to writing. She contributed numerous pieces to the *Westminster Review* throughout her literary career, but began publishing novels in 1858. Throughout her life she published seven novels, most notably *Middlemarch,* which was published in eight volumes from 1871-72. She died on December 22, 1880 of a throat infection and kidney disease.

The Lifted Veil

Give me no light, great Heaven, but such as turns
To energy of human fellowship;
No powers beyond the growing heritage
That makes completer manhood.

CHAPTER I

The time of my end approaches. I have lately been subject to attacks of angina pectoris; and in the ordinary course of things, my physician tells me, I may fairly hope that my life will not be protracted many months. Unless, then, I am cursed with an exceptional physical constitution, as I am cursed with an exceptional mental character, I shall not much longer groan under the wearisome burthen of this earthly existence. If it were to be otherwise—if I were to live on to the age most men desire and provide for—I should for once have known whether the miseries of delusive expectation can outweigh the miseries of true provision. For I foresee when I shall die, and everything that will happen in my last moments.

Just a month from this day, on September 20, 1850, I shall be sitting in this chair, in this study, at ten o'clock at night, longing to die, weary of incessant insight and foresight, without delusions and without hope. Just as I am watching a tongue of blue flame rising in the fire, and my lamp is burning low, the horrible contraction will begin at my chest. I shall only have time to reach the bell, and pull it violently, before the sense of suffocation will come. No one will answer my bell. I know why. My two servants are lovers, and will have quarrelled. My housekeeper will have rushed out of the house in a fury, two hours before, hoping that Perry will believe she has gone to drown herself. Perry is alarmed at last, and is gone out after her. The little scullery-maid is asleep on a bench: she never answers the bell; it does not wake her. The sense of suffocation increases: my lamp goes out with a horrible stench: I make a great effort, and snatch at the bell again. I long for life, and there is no help. I thirsted for the unknown: the thirst is gone. O God, let me stay with the known, and be weary of it: I am content. Agony of pain and suffocation—and all the while the earth, the fields, the pebbly brook at the bottom of the rookery, the fresh scent after the rain, the light of the morning through my chamber-window, the warmth of the hearth after the frosty air—will darkness close over them for ever?
Darkness—darkness—no pain—nothing but darkness: but I am passing on and on through the darkness: my thought stays in the darkness, but always with a sense of moving onward . . .

Before that time comes, I wish to use my last hours of ease and strength in telling the strange story of my experience. I have never fully unbosomed myself to any human being; I have never been encouraged to trust much in the sympathy of my fellow-men. But we have all a chance of meeting with some pity, some tenderness, some charity, when we are dead: it is the living only who cannot be forgiven—the living only from whom men's indulgence and reverence are held off, like the rain by the hard east wind. While the heart beats, bruise it— it is your only opportunity; while the eye can still turn towards you with moist, timid entreaty, freeze it with an icy unanswering gaze; while the ear, that delicate messenger to the inmost sanctuary of the soul, can still take in the tones of kindness, put it off with hard civility, or sneering compliment, or envious affectation of indifference; while the creative brain can still throb with the sense of injustice, with the yearning for brotherly recognition—make haste—oppress it with your ill-considered judgements, your trivial comparisons, your careless misrepresentations. The heart will by and by be still—"ubi saeva indignatio ulterius cor lacerare nequit"; the eye will cease to entreat; the ear will be deaf; the brain will have ceased from all wants as well as from all work. Then your charitable speeches may find vent; then you may remember and pity the toil and the struggle and the failure; then you may give due honour to the work achieved; then you may find extenuation for errors, and may consent to bury them.

That is a trivial schoolboy text; why do I dwell on it? It has little reference to me, for I shall leave no works behind me for men to honour. I have no near relatives who will make up, by weeping over my grave, for the wounds they inflicted on me when I was among them. It is only the story of my life that will perhaps win a little more sympathy from strangers when I am dead, than I ever believed it would obtain from my friends while I was living.

My childhood perhaps seems happier to me than it really was, by contrast with all the after-years. For then the curtain of the future was as impenetrable to me as to other children: I had all their delight in the present hour, their sweet indefinite hopes for the morrow; and I had a tender mother: even now, after the dreary lapse of long years, a slight trace of sensation accompanies the remembrance of her caress as she held me on her knee—her arms round my little body, her cheek pressed on mine. I had a complaint of the eyes that made me blind for a little while, and she kept me on her knee from morning till night. That unequalled love soon vanished out of my life, and even to my childish consciousness it was as if that life had become more chill I rode my little white pony with the groom by my side as before, but there were no loving eyes looking at me as I mounted, no glad arms opened to me when I came back. Perhaps I missed my mother's love more than most children of seven or eight would have done, to whom the other pleasures of life remained as before; for I was certainly a very sensitive child. I remember still the mingled trepidation and delicious excitement with which I was affected by the tramping of the horses on the pavement in the echoing stables, by the loud resonance of the groom's voices, by the booming bark of the dogs as my father's carriage thundered under the archway of the courtyard, by the din of the gong as it gave notice of luncheon and dinner. The measured tramp of soldiery which I sometimes heard—for my father's house lay near a county town where there were large barracks—made me sob and tremble; and yet when they were gone past, I longed for them to come back again.

I fancy my father thought me an odd child, and had little fondness for me; though he was very careful in fulfilling what he regarded as a parent's duties. But he was already past the middle of life, and I was not his only son. My mother had been his second wife, and he was five-and-forty when he married her. He was a firm, unbending, intensely orderly man, in root and stem a banker, but with a flourishing graft of the active landholder, aspiring to county influence: one of those people who are always like themselves from day to day, who are uninfluenced by the weather, and neither know melancholy nor high spirits. I held him in great awe, and appeared more timid and sensitive in his presence than at other times; a circumstance which, perhaps, helped to confirm him in the intention to educate me on a different plan from the prescriptive one with which he had complied in the case of my elder brother, already a tall youth at Eton. My brother was to be his representative and successor; he must go to Eton and Oxford, for the sake of making connexions, of course: my father was not a man to underrate the bearing of Latin satirists or Greek dramatists on the attainment of an aristocratic position. But, intrinsically, he had slight esteem for "those dead but sceptred spirits"; having qualified himself for forming an independent opinion by reading Potter's Æschylus, and dipping into Francis's Horace. To this negative view he added a positive one, derived from a recent connexion with mining speculations; namely, that a scientific education was the really useful training for a younger son. Moreover, it was clear that a shy, sensitive boy like me was not fit to encounter the rough experience of a public school. Mr. Letherall had said so very decidedly. Mr. Letherall was a large man in spectacles, who one day took my small head between his large hands, and pressed it here and there in an exploratory, auspicious manner—then placed each of his great thumbs on my temples, and pushed me a little way from him, and stared at me with glittering spectacles. The contemplation appeared to displease him, for he frowned sternly, and said to my father, drawing his thumbs across my eyebrows—

"The deficiency is there, sir—there; and here," he added, touching the upper sides of my head, "here is the excess. That must be brought out, sir, and this must be laid to sleep."

I was in a state of tremor, partly at the vague idea that I was the object of reprobation, partly in the agitation of my first hatred—hatred of this big, spectacled man, who pulled my head about as if he wanted to buy and cheapen it.

I am not aware how much Mr. Letherall had to do with the system afterwards adopted towards me, but it was presently clear that private tutors, natural history, science, and the modern languages, were the appliances by which the defects of my organization were to be remedied. I was very stupid about machines, so I was to be greatly occupied with them; I had no memory for classification, so it was particularly necessary that I should study systematic zoology and botany; I was hungry for human deeds and humane motions, so I was to be plentifully crammed with the mechanical powers, the elementary bodies, and the phenomena of electricity and magnetism. A better-constituted boy would certainly have profited under my intelligent tutors, with their scientific apparatus; and would, doubtless, have found the phenomena of electricity and magnetism as fascinating as I was, every Thursday, assured they were. As it was, I could have paired off, for ignorance of whatever was taught me, with the worst Latin scholar that was ever turned out of a classical academy. I read Plutarch, and Shakespeare, and Don Quixote by the sly, and supplied myself in that way with wandering thoughts, while my tutor was assuring me that "an improved man, as distinguished from an ignorant one, was a man who knew the reason why water ran downhill." I had no desire to be this improved man; I was glad of the running water; I could watch it and listen to it gurgling among the pebbles, and bathing the bright green water-plants, by the hour together. I did not want to know why it ran; I had perfect confidence that there were good reasons for what was so very beautiful.

There is no need to dwell on this part of my life. I have said enough to indicate that my nature was of the sensitive, unpractical order, and that it grew up in an uncongenial medium, which could never foster it into happy, healthy development. When I was sixteen I was sent to Geneva to complete my course of education; and the change was a very happy one to me, for the first sight of the Alps, with the setting sun on them, as we descended the Jura, seemed to me like an entrance into heaven; and the three years of my life there were spent in a perpetual sense of exaltation, as if from a draught of delicious wine, at the presence of Nature in all her awful loveliness. You will think, perhaps, that I must have been a poet, from this early sensibility to Nature. But my lot was not so happy as that. A poet pours forth his song and believes in the listening ear and answering soul, to which his song will be floated sooner or later. But the poet's sensibility without his voice—the poet's sensibility that finds no vent but in silent tears on the sunny bank, when the noonday light sparkles on the water, or in an inward shudder at the sound of harsh human tones, the sight of a cold human eye—this dumb passion brings with it a fatal solitude of soul in the society of one's fellow-men. My least solitary moments were those in which I pushed off in my boat, at evening, towards the centre of the lake; it seemed to me that the sky, and the glowing mountain-tops, and the wide blue water, surrounded me with a cherishing love such as no human face had shed on me since my mother's love had vanished out of my life. I used to do as Jean Jacques did—lie down in my boat and let it glide where it would, while I looked up at the departing glow leaving
one mountain-top after the other, as if the prophet's chariot of fire were

passing over them on its way to the home of light. Then, when the white summits were all sad and corpse-like, I had to push homeward, for I was under careful surveillance, and was allowed no late wanderings. This disposition of mine was not favourable to the formation of intimate friendships among the numerous youths of my own age who are always to be found studying at Geneva. Yet I made one such friendship; and, singularly enough, it was with a youth whose intellectual tendencies were the very reverse of my own. I shall call him Charles Meunier; his real surname—an English one, for he was of English extraction— having since become celebrated. He was an orphan, who lived on a miserable pittance while he pursued the medical studies for which he had a special genius. Strange! that with my vague mind, susceptible and unobservant, hating inquiry and given up to contemplation, I should have been drawn towards a youth whose strongest passion was science. But the bond was not an intellectual one; it came from a source that can happily blend the stupid with the brilliant, the dreamy with the practical: it came from community of feeling. Charles was poor and ugly, derided by Genevese gamins, and not acceptable in drawing-rooms. I saw that he was isolated, as I was, though from a different cause, and, stimulated by a sympathetic resentment, I made timid advances towards him. It is enough to say that there sprang up as much comradeship between us as our different habits would allow; and in Charles's rare holidays we went up the Salève together, or took the boat to Vevay, while I listened dreamily to the monologues in which he unfolded his bold conceptions of future experiment and discovery. I mingled them confusedly in my thought with glimpses of blue water and delicate floating cloud, with the notes of birds and the distant glitter of the glacier. He knew quite well that my mind was half absent, yet he liked to talk to me in this way; for don't we talk of our hopes and our projects even to dogs and birds, when they love us? I have mentioned this one friendship because of its connexion with a strange and terrible scene which I shall have to narrate in my subsequent life.

This happier life at Geneva was put an end to by a severe illness, which is partly a blank to me, partly a time of dimly-remembered suffering, with the presence of my father by my bed from time to time. Then came the languid monotony of convalescence, the days gradually breaking into variety and distinctness as my strength enabled me to take longer and longer drives. On one of these more vividly remembered days, my father said to me, as he sat beside my sofa—

"When you are quite well enough to travel, Latimer, I shall take you home with me. The journey will amuse you and do you good, for I shall go through the Tyrol and Austria, and you will see many new places. Our neighbours, the Filmores, are come; Alfred will join us at Basle, and we shall all go together to Vienna, and back by Prague" . . .

My father was called away before he had finished his sentence, and he left my mind resting on the word Prague, with a strange sense that a new and wondrous scene was breaking upon me: a city under the broad sunshine, that seemed to me as if it were the summer sunshine of a long-past century arrested in its course—unrefreshed for ages by dews of night, or the rushing rain-cloud; scorching the dusty, weary, time-eaten grandeur of a people doomed to live on in the stale repetition of memories, like deposed and superannuated kings in their regal gold-inwoven tatters. The city looked so thirsty that the broad river seemed to me a sheet of metal; and the blackened statues, as I passed under their blank gaze, along the unending bridge, with their ancient garments and their saintly crowns, seemed to me the real inhabitants and owners of this place, while the busy, trivial men and women, hurrying to and fro, were a swarm of ephemeral visitants infesting it for a day. It is such grim, stony beings as these, I thought, who are the fathers of ancient faded children, in those tanned time-fretted dwellings that crowd the steep before me; who pay their court in the worn and crumbling pomp of the palace which stretches its monotonous length on the height; who worship wearily in the stifling air of the churches, urged by no fear or hope, but compelled by their doom to be ever old and undying, to live on in the rigidity of habit, as they live on in perpetual midday, without the repose of night or the new birth of morning.

A stunning clang of metal suddenly thrilled through me, and I became conscious of the objects in my room again: one of the fire-irons had fallen as Pierre opened the door to bring me my draught. My heart was palpitating violently, and I begged Pierre to leave my draught beside me; I would take it presently.

As soon as I was alone again, I began to ask myself whether I had been sleeping. Was this a dream—this wonderfully distinct vision—minute in its distinctness down to a patch of rainbow light on the pavement, transmitted through a coloured lamp in the shape of a star—of a strange city, quite unfamiliar to my imagination? I had seen no picture of Prague: it lay in my mind as a mere name, with vaguely-remembered historical associations—ill-defined memories of imperial grandeur and religious wars.

Nothing of this sort had ever occurred in my dreaming experience before, for I had often been humiliated because my dreams were only saved from being utterly disjointed and commonplace by the frequent terrors of nightmare. But I could not believe that I had been asleep, for I remembered distinctly the gradual breaking-in of the vision upon me, like the new images in a dissolving view, or the growing distinctness of the landscape as the sun lifts up the veil of the morning mist. And while I was conscious of this incipient vision, I was also conscious that Pierre came to tell my father Mr. Filmore was waiting for him, and that my father hurried out of the room. No, it was not a dream; was it—the thought was full of tremulous exultation—was it the poet's nature in me, hitherto only a troubled yearning sensibility, now manifesting itself suddenly as spontaneous creation? Surely it was in this way that Homer saw the plain of Troy, that Dante saw the abodes of the departed, that Milton saw the earthward flight of the Tempter. Was it that my illness had wrought some happy change in my organization—given a firmer tension to my nerves—carried off some dull obstruction? I had often read of such effects—in works of fiction at least. Nay; in genuine biographies I had read of the subtilizing or exalting influence of some diseases on the mental powers. Did not Novalis feel his inspiration intensified under the progress of consumption?

When my mind had dwelt for some time on this blissful idea, it seemed to me that I might perhaps test it by an exertion of my will. The vision had begun when my father was speaking of our going to Prague. I did not for a moment believe it was really a representation of that city; I believed—I hoped it was a picture that my newly liberated genius had painted in fiery haste, with the colours snatched from lazy memory. Suppose I were to fix my mind on some other place—Venice, for example, which was far more familiar to my imagination than Prague: perhaps the same sort of result would follow. I concentrated my thoughts on Venice; I stimulated my imagination with poetic memories, and strove to feel myself present in Venice, as I had felt myself present in Prague. But in vain. I was only colouring the Canaletto engravings that hung in my old bedroom at home; the picture was a shifting one, my mind wandering uncertainly in search of more vivid images; I could see no accident of form or shadow without conscious labour after the necessary conditions. It was all prosaic effort, not rapt passivity, such as I had experienced half an hour before. I was discouraged; but I remembered that inspiration was fitful.

For several days I was in a state of excited expectation, watching for a recurrence of my new gift. I sent my thoughts ranging over my world of knowledge, in the hope that they would find some object which would send a reawakening vibration through my slumbering genius. But no; my world remained as dim as ever, and that flash of strange light refused to come again, though I watched for it with palpitating eagerness.

My father accompanied me every day in a drive, and a gradually lengthening walk as my powers of walking increased; and one evening he had agreed to come and fetch me at twelve the next day, that we might go together to select a musical box, and other purchases rigorously demanded of a rich Englishman visiting Geneva. He was one of the most punctual of men and bankers, and I was always nervously anxious to be quite ready for him at the appointed time. But, to my surprise, at a quarter past twelve he had not appeared. I felt all the impatience of a convalescent who has nothing particular to do, and who has just taken a tonic in the prospect of immediate exercise that would carry off the stimulus.

Unable to sit still and reserve my strength, I walked up and down the room, looking out on the current of the Rhone, just where it leaves the dark-blue lake; but thinking all the while of the possible causes that could detain my father.

Suddenly I was conscious that my father was in the room, but not alone: there were two persons with him. Strange! I had heard no footstep, I had not seen the door open; but I saw my father, and at his right hand our neighbour Mrs. Filmore, whom I remembered very well, though I had not seen her for five years. She was a commonplace middle-aged woman, in silk and cashmere; but the lady on the left of my father was not more than twenty, a tall, slim, willowy figure, with luxuriant blond hair, arranged in cunning braids and folds that looked almost too massive for the slight figure and the small-featured, thin-lipped face they crowned. But the face had not a girlish expression: the features were sharp, the pale grey eyes at once acute, restless, and sarcastic. They were fixed on me in half-smiling curiosity, and I felt a painful sensation as if a sharp wind were cutting me. The pale-green dress, and the green leaves that seemed to form a border about her pale blond hair, made me think of a Water-Nixie—for my mind was full of German lyrics, and this pale, fatal-eyed woman, with the green weeds, looked like a birth from some cold sedgy stream, the daughter of an aged river.

"Well, Latimer, you thought me long," my father said . . .

But while the last word was in my ears, the whole group vanished, and there was nothing between me and the Chinese printed folding-screen that stood before the door. I was cold and trembling; I could only totter forward and throw myself on the sofa. This strange new power had manifested itself again . . . But was it a power? Might it not rather be a disease—a sort of intermittent delirium, concentrating my energy of brain into moments of unhealthy activity, and leaving my saner hours all the more barren? I felt a dizzy sense of unreality in what my eye rested on; I grasped the bell convulsively, like one trying to free himself from nightmare, and rang it twice. Pierre came with a look of alarm in his face.

"Monsieur ne se trouve pas bien?" he said anxiously.

"I'm tired of waiting, Pierre," I said, as distinctly and emphatically as I could, like a man determined to be sober in spite of wine; "I'm afraid something has happened to my father—he's usually so punctual. Run to the Hôtel des Bergues and see if he is there."

Pierre left the room at once, with a soothing "Bien, Monsieur"; and I felt the better for this scene of simple, waking prose. Seeking to calm myself still further, I went into my bedroom, adjoining the salon, and opened a case of eau-de-Cologne; took out a bottle; went through the process of taking out the cork very neatly, and then rubbed the reviving spirit over my hands and forehead, and under my nostrils, drawing a new delight from the scent because I had procured it by slow details of labour, and by no strange sudden madness. Already I had begun to taste something of the horror that belongs to the lot of a human being whose nature is not adjusted to simple human conditions.

Still enjoying the scent, I returned to the salon, but it was not unoccupied, as it had been before I left it. In front of the Chinese folding-screen there was my father, with Mrs. Filmore on his right hand, and on his left—the slim, blond-haired girl, with the keen face and the keen eyes fixed on me in half-smiling curiosity.

"Well, Latimer, you thought me long," my father said . . .

I heard no more, felt no more, till I became conscious that I was lying with my head low on the sofa, Pierre, and my father by my side. As soon as I was thoroughly revived, my father left the room, and presently returned, saying—

"I've been to tell the ladies how you are, Latimer. They were waiting in the next room. We shall put off our shopping expedition to-day."

Presently he said, "That young lady is Bertha Grant, Mrs. Filmore's orphan niece. Filmore has adopted her, and she lives with them, so you will have her for a neighbour when we go home—perhaps for a near relation; for there is a tenderness between her and Alfred, I suspect, and I should be gratified by the match, since Filmore means to provide for her in every way as if she were his daughter. It had not occurred to me that you knew nothing about her living with the Filmores."

He made no further allusion to the fact of my having fainted at the moment of seeing her, and I would not for the world have told him the reason: I shrank from the idea of disclosing to any one what might be regarded as a pitiable peculiarity, most of all from betraying it to my father, who would have suspected my sanity ever after.

I do not mean to dwell with particularity on the details of my experience. I have described these two cases at length, because they had definite, clearly traceable results in my after-lot.

Shortly after this last occurrence—I think the very next day—I began to be aware of a phase in my abnormal sensibility, to which, from the languid and slight nature of my intercourse with others since my illness, I had not been alive before. This was the obtrusion on my mind of the mental process going forward in first one person, and then another, with whom I happened to be in contact: the vagrant, frivolous ideas and emotions of some uninteresting acquaintance— Mrs. Filmore, for example—would force themselves on my consciousness like an importunate, ill-played musical instrument, or the loud activity of an imprisoned insect. But this unpleasant sensibility was fitful, and left me moments of rest, when the souls of my companions were once more shut out from me, and

I felt a relief such as silence brings to wearied nerves. I might have believed this importunate insight to be merely a diseased activity of the imagination, but that my prevision of incalculable words and actions proved it to have a fixed relation to the mental process in other minds. But this superadded consciousness, wearying and annoying enough when it urged on me the trivial experience of indifferent people, became an intense pain and grief when it seemed to be opening to me the souls of those who were in a close relation to me—when the rational talk, the graceful attentions, the wittily-turned phrases, and the kindly deeds, which used to make the web of their characters, were seen as if thrust asunder by a microscopic vision, that showed all the intermediate frivolities, all the suppressed egoism, all the struggling chaos of puerilities, meanness, vague capricious memories, and indolent make-shift thoughts, from which human words and deeds emerge like leaflets covering a fermenting heap.

At Basle we were joined by my brother Alfred, now a handsome, self-confident man of six-and-twenty—a thorough contrast to my fragile, nervous, ineffectual self. I believe I was held to have a sort of half-womanish, half-ghostly beauty; for the portrait-painters, who are thick as weeds at Geneva, had often asked me to sit to them, and I had been the model of a dying minstrel in a fancy picture. But I thoroughly disliked my own physique and nothing but the belief that it was a condition of poetic genius would have reconciled me to it. That brief hope was quite fled, and I saw in my face now nothing but the stamp of a morbid organization, framed for passive suffering—too feeble for the sublime resistance of poetic production. Alfred, from whom I had been almost constantly separated, and who, in his present stage of character and appearance, came before me as a perfect stranger, was bent on being extremely friendly and brother-like to me. He had the superficial kindness of a good-humoured, self-satisfied nature, that fears no rivalry, and has encountered no contrarieties. I am not sure that my disposition was good enough for me to have been quite free from envy towards him, even if our desires had not clashed, and if I had been in the healthy human condition which admits of generous confidence and charitable construction. There must always have been an antipathy between our natures. As it was, he became in a few weeks an object of intense hatred to me; and when he entered the room, still more when he spoke, it was as if a sensation of grating metal had set my teeth on edge. My diseased consciousness was more intensely and continually occupied with his thoughts and emotions, than with those of any other person who came in my way. I was perpetually exasperated with the petty promptings of his conceit and his love of patronage, with his self-complacent belief in Bertha Grant's passion for him, with his half-pitying contempt for me— seen not in the ordinary indications of intonation and phrase and slight action, which an acute and suspicious mind is on the watch for, but in all their naked skinless complication.

For we were rivals, and our desires clashed, though he was not aware of it. I have said nothing yet of the effect Bertha Grant produced in me on a nearer acquaintance. That effect was chiefly determined by the fact that she made the only exception, among all the human beings about me, to my unhappy gift of insight. About Bertha I was always in a state of uncertainty: I could watch the expression of her face, and speculate on its meaning; I could ask for her opinion with the real interest of ignorance; I could listen for her words and watch for her smile with hope and fear: she had for me the fascination of an unravelled destiny. I say it was this fact that chiefly determined the strong effect she produced on me: for, in the abstract, no womanly character could seem to have less affinity for that of a shrinking, romantic, passionate youth than Bertha's. She was keen, sarcastic, unimaginative, prematurely cynical, remaining critical and unmoved in the most impressive scenes, inclined to dissect all my favourite poems, and especially contemptous towards the German lyrics which were my pet literature at that time. To this moment I am unable to define my feeling towards her: it was not ordinary boyish admiration, for she was the very opposite, even to the colour of her hair, of the ideal woman who still remained to me the type of loveliness; and she was without that enthusiasm for the great and good, which, even at the moment of her strongest dominion over me, I should have declared to be the highest element of character. But there is no tyranny more complete than that which a self-centred negative nature exercises over a morbidly sensitive nature perpetually craving sympathy and support. The most independent people feel the effect of a man's silence in heightening their value for his opinion—feel an additional triumph in conquering the reverence of a critic habitually captious and satirical: no wonder, then, that an enthusiastic self-distrusting youth should watch and wait before the closed secret of a sarcastic woman's face, as if it were the shrine of the doubtfully benignant deity who ruled his destiny. For a young enthusiast is unable to imagine the total negation in another mind of the emotions which are stirring his own: they may be feeble, latent, inactive, he thinks, but they are there—they may be called forth; sometimes, in moments of happy hallucination, he believes they may be there in all the greater strength because he sees no outward sign of them. And this effect, as I have intimated, was heightened to its utmost intensity in me, because Bertha was the only being who remained for me in the mysterious seclusion of soul that renders such youthful delusion possible. Doubtless there was another sort of fascination at work—that subtle physical attraction which delights in cheating our psychological predictions, and in compelling the men who paint sylphs, to fall in love with some bonne et brave femme, heavy-heeled and freckled.

Bertha's behaviour towards me was such as to encourage all my illusions, to heighten my boyish passion, and make me more and more dependent on her smiles. Looking back with my present wretched knowledge, I conclude that her vanity and love of power were intensely gratified by the belief that I had fainted on first seeing her purely from the strong impression her person had produced on me. The most prosaic woman likes to believe herself the object of a violent, a poetic passion; and without a grain of romance in her, Bertha had that spirit of intrigue which gave piquancy to the idea that the brother of the man she meant to marry was dying with love and jealousy for her sake. That she meant to marry my brother, was what at that time I did not believe; for though he was assiduous in his attentions to her, and I knew well enough that both he and my father had made up their minds to this result, there was not yet an understood engagement—there had been no explicit declaration; and Bertha habitually, while she flirted with my brother, and accepted his homage in a way that implied to him a thorough recognition of its intention, made me believe, by the subtlest looks and phrases—feminine nothings which could never be quoted against her—that he was really the object of her secret ridicule; that she thought him, as I did, a coxcomb, whom she would have pleasure in disappointing. Me she openly petted in my brother's presence, as if I were too young and sickly ever to be thought of as a lover; and that was the view he took of me. But I believe she must inwardly have delighted in the tremors into which she threw me by the coaxing way in which she patted my curls, while she laughed at my quotations. Such caresses were always given in the presence of our friends; for when we were alone together, she affected a much greater distance towards me, and now and then took the opportunity, by words or slight actions, to stimulate my foolish timid hope that she really preferred me. And why should she not follow her inclination? I was not in so advantageous a position as my brother, but I had fortune, I was not a year younger than she was, and she was an heiress, who would soon be of age to decide for herself.

The fluctuations of hope and fear, confined to this one channel, made each day in her presence a delicious torment. There was one deliberate act of hers which especially helped to intoxicate me. When we were at Vienna her twentieth birthday occurred, and as she was very fond of ornaments, we all took the opportunity of the splendid jewellers' shops in that Teutonic Paris to purchase her a birthday present of jewellery. Mine, naturally, was the least expensive; it was an opal ring—the opal was my favourite stone, because it seems to blush and turn pale as if it had a soul. I told Bertha so when I gave it her, and said that it was an emblem of the poetic nature, changing with the changing light of heaven and of woman's eyes. In the evening she appeared elegantly dressed, and wearing conspicuously all the birthday presents except mine. I looked eagerly at her fingers, but saw no opal. I had no opportunity of noticing this to her during the evening; but the next day, when I found her seated near the window alone, after breakfast, I said, "You scorn to wear my poor opal. I should have remembered that you despised poetic natures, and should have given you coral, or turquoise, or some other opaque unresponsive stone." "Do I despise it?" she answered, taking hold of a delicate gold chain which she always wore round her neck and drawing out the end from her bosom with my ring hanging to it; "it hurts me a little, I can tell you," she said, with her usual dubious smile, "to wear it in that secret place; and since your poetical nature is so stupid as to prefer a more public position, I shall not endure the pain any longer."

She took off the ring from the chain and put it on her finger, smiling still, while the blood rushed to my cheeks, and I could not trust myself to say a word of entreaty that she would keep the ring where it was before.

I was completely fooled by this, and for two days shut myself up in my own room whenever Bertha was absent, that I might intoxicate myself afresh with the thought of this scene and all it implied.

I should mention that during these two months—which seemed a long life to me from the novelty and intensity of the pleasures and pains I underwent—my diseased anticipation in other people's consciousness continued to torment me; now it was my father, and now my brother, now Mrs. Filmore or her husband, and now our German courier, whose stream of thought rushed upon me like a ringing in the ears not to be got rid of, though it allowed my own impulses and ideas to continue their uninterrupted course. It was like a preternaturally heightened sense of hearing, making audible to one a roar of sound where others find perfect stillness. The weariness and disgust of this involuntary intrusion into other souls was counteracted only by my ignorance of Bertha, and my growing passion for her; a passion enormously stimulated, if not produced, by that ignorance. She was my oasis of mystery in the dreary desert of knowledge. I had never allowed my diseased condition to betray itself, or to drive me into any unusual speech or action, except once, when, in a moment of peculiar bitterness against my brother, I had forestalled some words which I knew he was going to utter—a clever observation, which he had prepared beforehand. He had occasionally a slightly affected hesitation in his speech, and when he paused an instant after the second word, my impatience and jealousy impelled me to continue the speech for him, as if it were something we had both learned by rote. He coloured and looked astonished, as well as annoyed; and the words had no sooner escaped my lips than I felt a shock of alarm lest such an anticipation of words—very far from being words of course, easy to divine—should have betrayed me as an exceptional being, a sort of quiet energumen, whom every one, Bertha above all, would shudder at and avoid. But I magnified, as usual, the impression any word or deed of mine could produce on others; for no one gave any sign of having noticed my interruption as more than a rudeness, to be forgiven me on the score of my feeble nervous condition.

While this superadded consciousness of the actual was almost constant with me, I had never had a recurrence of that distinct prevision which I have described in relation to my first interview with Bertha; and I was waiting with eager curiosity to know whether or not my vision of Prague would prove to have been an instance of the same kind. A few days after the incident of the opal ring, we were paying one of our frequent visits to the Lichtenberg Palace. I could never look at many pictures in succession; for pictures, when they are at all powerful, affect me so strongly that one or two exhaust all my capability of contemplation. This morning I had been looking at Giorgione's picture of the cruel-eyed woman, said to be a likeness of Lucrezia Borgia. I had stood long alone before it, fascinated by the terrible reality of that cunning, relentless face, till I felt a strange poisoned sensation, as if I had long been inhaling a fatal odour, and was just beginning to be conscious of its effects. Perhaps even then I should not have moved away, if the rest of the party had not returned to this room, and announced that they were going to the Belvedere Gallery to settle a bet which had arisen between my brother and Mr. Filmore about a portrait. I followed them dreamily, and was hardly alive to what occurred till they had all gone up to the gallery, leaving me below; for I refused to come within sight of another picture that day. I made my way to the Grand Terrace, since it was agreed that we should saunter in the gardens when the dispute had been decided. I had been sitting here a short space, vaguely conscious of trim gardens, with a city and green hills in the distance, when, wishing to avoid the proximity of the sentinel, I rose and walked down the broad stone steps, intending to seat myself farther on in the gardens. Just as I reached the gravel-walk, I felt an arm slipped within mine, and a light hand gently pressing my wrist. In the same instant a strange intoxicating numbness passed over me, like the continuance or climax of the sensation I was still feeling from the gaze of Lucrezia Borgia. The gardens, the summer sky, the consciousness of Bertha's arm being within mine, all vanished, and I seemed to be suddenly in darkness, out of which there gradually broke a dim firelight, and I felt myself sitting in my father's leather chair in the library at home. I knew the fireplace—the dogs for the wood-fire—the black marble chimney-piece with the white marble medallion of the dying Cleopatra in the centre. Intense and hopeless misery was pressing on my soul; the light became stronger, for Bertha was entering with a candle in her hand—Bertha, my wife—with cruel eyes, with green jewels and green leaves on her white ball-dress; every hateful thought within her present to me . . . "Madman, idiot! why don't you kill yourself, then?" It was a moment of hell. I saw into her pitiless soul—saw its barren worldliness, its scorching hate—and felt it clothe me round like an air I was obliged to breathe. She came with her candle and stood over me with a bitter smile of contempt; I saw the great emerald brooch on her bosom, a studded serpent with diamond eyes. I shuddered—I despised this woman with the barren soul and mean thoughts; but I felt helpless before her, as if she clutched my bleeding heart, and would clutch it till the last drop of life-blood ebbed away. She was my wife, and we hated each other. Gradually the hearth, the dim library, the candle-light disappeared—seemed to melt away into a background of light, the green serpent with the diamond eyes remaining a dark image on the retina. Then I had a sense of my eyelids quivering, and the living daylight broke in upon me; I saw gardens, and heard voices; I was seated on the steps of the Belvedere Terrace, and my friends were round me.

The tumult of mind into which I was thrown by this hideous vision made me ill for several days, and prolonged our stay at Vienna. I shuddered with horror as the scene recurred to me; and it recurred constantly, with all its minutiæ, as if they had been burnt into my memory; and yet, such is the madness of the human heart under the influence of its immediate desires,

84

I felt a wild hell-braving joy that Bertha was to be mine; for the fulfilment of my former prevision concerning her first appearance before me, left me little hope that this last hideous glimpse of the future was the mere diseased play of my own mind, and had no relation to external realities. One thing alone I looked towards as a possible means of casting doubt on my terrible conviction—the discovery that my vision of Prague had been false—and Prague was the next city on our route.

Meanwhile, I was no sooner in Bertha's society again than I was as completely under her sway as before. What if I saw into the heart of Bertha, the matured woman—Bertha, my wife? Bertha, the girl, was a fascinating secret to me still: I trembled under her touch; I felt the witchery of her presence; I yearned to be assured of her love. The fear of poison is feeble against the sense of thirst. Nay, I was just as jealous of my brother as before—just as much irritated by his small patronizing ways; for my pride, my diseased sensibility, were there as they had always been, and winced as inevitably under every offence as my eye winced from an intruding mote. The future, even when brought within the compass of feeling by a vision that made me shudder, had still no more than the force of an idea, compared with the force of present emotion—of my love for Bertha, of my dislike and jealousy towards my brother.

It is an old story, that men sell themselves to the tempter, and sign a bond with their blood, because it is only to take effect at a distant day; then rush on to snatch the cup their souls thirst after with an impulse not the less savage because there is a dark shadow beside them for evermore. There is no short cut, no patent tram-road, to wisdom: after all the centuries of invention, the soul's path lies through the thorny wilderness which must be still trodden in solitude, with bleeding feet, with sobs for help, as it was trodden by them of old time.

My mind speculated eagerly on the means by which I should become my brother's successful rival, for I was still too timid, in my ignorance of Bertha's actual feeling, to venture on any step that would urge from her an avowal of it. I thought I should gain confidence even for this, if my vision of Prague proved to have been veracious; and yet, the horror of that certitude! Behind the slim girl Bertha, whose words and looks I watched for, whose touch was bliss, there stood continually that Bertha with the fuller form, the harder eyes, the more rigid mouth—with the barren, selfish soul laid bare; no longer a fascinating secret, but a measured fact, urging itself perpetually on my unwilling sight. Are you unable to give me your sympathy—you who react this? Are you unable to imagine this double consciousness at work within me, flowing on like two parallel streams which never mingle their waters and blend into a common hue? Yet you must have known something of the presentiments that spring from an insight at war with passion; and my visions were only like presentiments intensified to horror. You have known the powerlessness of ideas before the might of impulse; and my visions, when once they had passed into memory, were mere ideas—pale shadows that beckoned in vain, while my hand was grasped by the living and the loved.

In after-days I thought with bitter regret that if I had foreseen something more or something different—if instead of that hideous vision which poisoned the passion it could not destroy, or if even along with it I could have had a foreshadowing of that moment when I looked on my brother's face for the last time, some softening influence would have been shed over my feeling towards him: pride and hatred would surely have been subdued into pity, and the record of those hidden sins would have been shortened. But this is one of the vain thoughts with which we men flatter ourselves. We try to believe that the egoism within us would have easily been melted, and that it was only the narrowness of our knowledge which hemmed in our generosity, our awe, our human piety, and hindered them from submerging our hard indifference to the sensations and emotions of our fellows. Our tenderness and self-renunciation seem strong when our egoism has had its day—when, after our mean striving for a triumph that is to be another's loss, the triumph comes suddenly, and we shudder at it, because it is held out by the chill hand of death.

Our arrival in Prague happened at night, and I was glad of this, for it seemed like a deferring of a terribly decisive moment, to be in the city for hours without seeing it. As we were not to remain long in Prague, but to go on speedily to Dresden, it was proposed that we should drive out the next morning and take a general view of the place, as well as visit some of its specially interesting spots, before the heat became oppressive—for we were in August, and the season was hot and dry. But it happened that the ladies were rather late at their morning toilet, and to my father's politely-repressed but perceptible annoyance, we were not in the carriage till the morning was far advanced. I thought with a sense of relief, as we entered the Jews' quarter, where we were to visit the old synagogue, that we should be kept in this flat, shut-up part of the city, until we should all be too tired and too warm to go farther, and so we should return without seeing more than the streets through which we had already passed. That would give me another day's suspense—suspense, the only form in which a fearful spirit knows the solace of hope. But, as I stood under the blackened, groined arches of that old synagogue, made dimly visible by the seven thin candles in the sacred lamp, while our Jewish cicerone reached down the Book of the Law, and read to us in its ancient tongue—I felt a shuddering impression that this strange building, with its shrunken lights, this surviving withered remnant of medieval Judaism, was of a piece with my vision. Those darkened dusty Christian saints, with their loftier arches and their larger candles, needed the consolatory scorn with which they might point to a more shrivelled death-in-life than their own.

As I expected, when we left the Jews' quarter the elders of our party wished to return to the hotel. But now, instead of rejoicing in this, as I had done beforehand, I felt a sudden overpowering impulse to go on at once to the bridge, and put an end to the suspense I had been wishing to protract. I declared, with unusual decision, that I would get out of the carriage and walk on alone; they might return without me. My father, thinking this merely a sample of my usual "poetic nonsense," objected that I should only do myself harm by walking in the heat; but when I persisted, he said angrily that I might follow my own absurd devices, but that Schmidt (our courier) must go with me. I assented to this, and set off with Schmidt towards the bridge. I had no sooner passed from under the archway of the grand old gate leading an to the bridge, than a trembling seized me, and I turned cold under the midday sun; yet I went on; I was in search of something—a small detail which I remembered with special intensity as part of my vision. There it was—the patch of rainbow light on the pavement transmitted through a lamp in the shape of a star.

CHAPTER II

Before the autumn was at an end, and while the brown leaves still stood thick on the beeches in our park, my brother and Bertha were engaged to each other, and it was understood that their marriage was to take place early in the next spring. In spite of the certainty I had felt from that moment on the bridge at Prague, that Bertha would one day be my wife, my constitutional timidity and distrust had continued to benumb me, and the words in which I had sometimes premeditated a confession of my love, had died away unuttered. The same conflict had gone on within me as before—the longing for an assurance of love from Bertha's lips, the dread lest a word of contempt and denial should fall upon me like a corrosive acid. What was the conviction of a distant necessity to me? I trembled under a present glance, I hungered after a present joy, I was clogged and chilled by a present fear. And so the days passed on: I witnessed Bertha's engagement and heard her marriage discussed as if I were under a conscious nightmare—knowing it was a dream that would vanish, but feeling stifled under the grasp of hard-clutching fingers.

When I was not in Bertha's presence—and I was with her very often, for she continued to treat me with a playful patronage that wakened no jealousy in my brother—I spent my time chiefly in wandering, in strolling, or taking long rides while the daylight lasted, and then shutting myself up with my unread books; for books had lost the power of chaining my attention. My self-consciousness was heightened to that pitch of intensity in which our own emotions take the form of a drama which urges itself imperatively on our contemplation, and we begin to weep, less under the sense of our suffering than at the thought of it. I felt a sort of pitying anguish over the pathos of my own lot: the lot of a being finely organized for pain, but with hardly any fibres that responded to pleasure—to whom the idea of future evil robbed the present of its joy, and for whom the idea of future good did not still the uneasiness of a present yearning or a present dread. I went dumbly through that stage of the poet's suffering, in which he feels the delicious pang of utterance, and makes an image of his sorrows.

I was left entirely without remonstrance concerning this dreamy way-ward life: I knew my father's thought about me: "That lad will never be good for anything in life: he may waste his years in an insignificant way on the income that falls to him: I shall not trouble myself about a career for him."

One mild morning in the beginning of November, it happened that I was standing outside the portico patting lazy old Cæsar, a Newfoundland almost blind with age, the only dog that ever took any notice of me—for the very dogs shunned me, and fawned on the happier people about me—when the groom brought up my brother's horse which was to carry him to the hunt, and my brother himself appeared at the door, florid, broad-chested, and self-complacent, feeling what a good-natured fellow he was not to behave insolently to us all on the strength of his great advantages.

"Latimer, old boy," he said to me in a tone of compassionate cordiality, "what a pity it is you don't have a run with the hounds now and then! The finest thing in the world for low spirits!"

"Low spirits!" I thought bitterly, as he rode away; "that is the sort of phrase with which coarse, narrow natures like yours think to describe experience of which you can know no more than your horse knows. It is to such as you that the good of this world falls: ready dulness, healthy selfishness, good-tempered conceit—these are the keys to happiness."

The quick thought came, that my selfishness was even stronger than his—it was only a suffering selfishness instead of an enjoying one. But then, again, my exasperating insight into Alfred's self-complacent soul, his freedom from all the doubts and fears, the unsatisfied yearnings, the exquisite tortures of sensitiveness, that had made the web of my life, seemed to absolve me from all bonds towards him. This man needed no pity, no love; those fine influences would have been as little felt by him as the delicate white mist is felt by the rock it caresses. There was no evil in store for him: if he was not to marry Bertha, it would be because he had found a lot pleasanter to himself.

Mr. Filmore's house lay not more than half a mile beyond our own gates, and whenever I knew my brother was gone in another direction, I went there for the chance of finding Bertha at home. Later on in the day I walked thither. By a rare accident she was alone, and we walked out in the grounds together, for she seldom went on foot beyond the trimly-swept gravel-walks. I remember what a beautiful sylph she looked to me as the low November sun shone on her blond hair, and she tripped along teasing me with her usual light banter, to which I listened half fondly, half moodily; it was all the sign Bertha's mysterious inner self ever made to me. To-day perhaps, the moodiness predominated, for I had not yet shaken off the access of jealous hate which my brother had raised in me by his parting patronage. Suddenly I interrupted and startled her by saying, almost fiercely, "Bertha, how can you love Alfred?"

She looked at me with surprise for a moment, but soon her light smile came again, and she answered sarcastically, "Why do you suppose I love him?"

"How can you ask that, Bertha?"

"What! your wisdom thinks I must love the man I'm going to marry? The most unpleasant thing in the world. I should quarrel with him; I should be jealous of him; our ménage would be conducted in a very ill-bred manner. A little quiet contempt contributes greatly to the elegance of life."

"Bertha, that is not your real feeling. Why do you delight in trying to deceive me by inventing such cynical speeches?"

"I need never take the trouble of invention in order to deceive you, my small Tasso"—(that was the mocking name she usually gave me). "The easiest way to deceive a poet is to tell him the truth."

She was testing the validity of her epigram in a daring way, and for a moment the shadow of my vision—the Bertha whose soul was no secret to me—passed between me and the radiant girl, the playful sylph whose feelings were a fascinating mystery. I suppose I must have shuddered, or betrayed in some other way my momentary chill of horror.

"Tasso!" she said, seizing my wrist, and peeping round into my face, "are you really beginning to discern what a heartless girl I am? Why, you are not half the poet I thought you were; you are actually capable of believing the truth about me."

The shadow passed from between us, and was no longer the object nearest to me. The girl whose light fingers grasped me, whose elfish charming face looked into mine—who, I thought, was betraying an interest in my feelings that she would not have directly avowed,—this warm breathing presence again possessed my senses and imagination like a returning siren melody which had been overpowered for an instant by the roar of threatening waves. It was a moment as delicious to me as the waking up to a consciousness of youth after a dream of middle age. I forgot everything but my passion, and said with swimming eyes—

"Bertha, shall you love me when we are first married? I wouldn't mind if you really loved me only for a little while."

Her look of astonishment, as she loosed my hand and started away from me, recalled me to a sense of my strange, my criminal indiscretion.

"Forgive me," I said, hurriedly, as soon as I could speak again; "I did not know what I was saying."

"Ah, Tasso's mad fit has come on, I see," she answered quietly, for she had recovered herself sooner than I had. "Let him go home and keep his head cool. I must go in, for the sun is setting."

I left her—full of indignation against myself. I had let slip words which, if she reflected on them, might rouse in her a suspicion of my abnormal mental condition—a suspicion which of all things I dreaded. And besides that, I was ashamed of the apparent baseness I had committed in uttering them to my brother's betrothed wife. I wandered home slowly, entering our park through a private gate instead of by the lodges. As I approached the house, I saw a man dashing off at full speed from the stable-yard across the park. Had any accident happened at home? No; perhaps it was only one of my father's peremptory business errands that required this headlong haste.

Nevertheless I quickened my pace without any distinct motive, and was soon at the house. I will not dwell on the scene I found there. My brother was dead—had been pitched from his horse, and killed on the spot by a concussion of the brain.

I went up to the room where he lay, and where my father was seated beside him with a look of rigid despair. I had shunned my father more than any one since our return home, for the radical antipathy between our natures made my insight into his inner self a constant affliction to me. But now, as I went up to him, and stood beside him in sad silence, I felt the presence of a new element that blended us as we had never been blent before. My father had been one of the most successful men in the money-getting world: he had had no sentimental sufferings, no illness. The heaviest trouble that had befallen him was the death of his first wife. But he married my mother soon after; and I remember he seemed exactly the same, to my keen childish observation, the week after her death as before. But now, at last, a sorrow had come—the sorrow of old age, which suffers the more from the crushing of its pride and its hopes, in proportion as the pride and hope are narrow and prosaic. His son was to have been married soon—would probably have stood for the borough at the next election. That son's existence was the best motive that could be alleged for making new purchases of land every year to round off the estate. It is a dreary thing onto live on doing the same things year after year, without knowing why we do them. Perhaps the tragedy of disappointed youth and passion is less piteous than the tragedy of disappointed age and worldliness.

As I saw into the desolation of my father's heart, I felt a movement of deep pity towards him, which was the beginning of a new affection—an affection that grew and strengthened in spite of the strange bitterness with which he regarded me in the first month or two after my brother's death. If it had not been for the softening influence of my compassion for him—the first deep compassion I had ever felt—I should have been stung by the perception that my father transferred the inheritance of an eldest son to me with a mortified sense that fate had compelled him to the unwelcome course of caring for me as an important being. It was only in spite of himself that he began to think of me with anxious regard. There is hardly any neglected child for whom death has made vacant a more favoured place, who will not understand what I mean.

Gradually, however, my new deference to his wishes, the effect of that patience which was born of my pity for him, won upon his affection, and he began to please himself with the endeavour to make me fill any brother's place as fully as my feebler personality would admit. I saw that the prospect which by and by presented itself of my becoming Bertha's husband was welcome to him, and he even contemplated in my case what he had not intended in my brother's—that his son and daughter-in-law should make one household with him. My softened feelings towards my father made this the happiest time I had known since childhood;—these last months in which I retained the delicious illusion of loving Bertha, of longing and doubting and hoping that she might love me. She behaved with a certain new consciousness and distance towards me after my brother's death; and I too was under a double constraint—that of delicacy towards my brother's memory and of anxiety as to the impression my abrupt words had left on her mind. But the additional screen this mutual reserve erected between us only brought me more completely under her power: no matter how empty the adytum, so that the veil be thick enough. So absolute is our soul's need of something hidden and uncertain for the maintenance of that doubt and hope and effort which are the breath of its life, that if the whole future were laid bare to us beyond to-day, the interest of all mankind would be bent on the hours that lie between; we should pant after the uncertainties of our one morning and our one afternoon; we should rush fiercely to the Exchange for our last possibility of speculation, of success, of disappointment: we should have a glut of political prophets foretelling a crisis or a no-crisis within the only twenty-four hours left open to prophecy. Conceive the condition of the human mind if all propositions whatsoever were self-evident except one, which was to become self-evident at the close of a summer's day, but in the meantime might be the subject of question, of hypothesis, of debate. Art and philosophy, literature and science, would fasten like bees on that one proposition which had the honey of probability in it, and be the more eager because their enjoyment would end with sunset. Our impulses, our spiritual activities, no more adjust themselves to the idea of their future nullity, than the beating of our heart, or the irritability of our muscles.

Bertha, the slim, fair-haired girl, whose present thoughts and emotions were an enigma to me amidst the fatiguing obviousness of the other minds around me, was as absorbing to me as a single unknown to-day—as a single hypothetic proposition to remain problematic till sunset; and all the cramped, hemmed-in belief and disbelief, trust and distrust, of my nature, welled out in this one narrow channel.

And she made me believe that she loved me. Without ever quitting her tone of badinage and playful superiority, she intoxicated me with the sense that I was necessary to her, that she was never at ease, unless I was near her, submitting to her playful tyranny. It costs a woman so little effort to beset us in this way! A half-repressed word, a moment's unexpected silence, even an easy fit of petulance on our account, will serve us as hashish for a long while. Out of the subtlest web of scarcely perceptible signs, she set me weaving the fancy that she had always unconsciously loved me better than Alfred, but that, with the ignorant fluttered sensibility of a young girl, she had been imposed on by the charm that lay for her in the distinction of being admired and chosen by a man who made so brilliant a figure in the world as my brother. She satirized herself in a very graceful way for her vanity and ambition. What was it to me that I had the light of my wretched provision on the fact that now it was I who possessed at least all but the personal part of my brother's advantages? Our sweet illusions are half of them conscious illusions, like effects of colour that we know to be made up of tinsel, broken glass, and rags.

We were married eighteen months after Alfred's death, one cold, clear morning in April, when there came hail and sunshine both together; and Bertha, in her white silk and pale-green leaves, and the pale hues of her hair and face, looked like the spirit of the morning. My father was happier than he had thought of being again: my marriage, he felt sure, would complete the desirable modification of my character, and make me practical and worldly enough to take my place in society among sane men. For he delighted in Bertha's tact and acuteness, and felt sure she would be mistress of me, and make me what she chose: I was only twenty-one, and madly in love with her. Poor father! He kept that hope a little while after our first year of marriage, and it was not quite extinct when paralysis came and saved him from utter disappointment.

I shall hurry through the rest of my story, not dwelling so much as I have hitherto done on my inward experience. When people are well known to each other, they talk rather of what befalls them externally, leaving their feelings and sentiments to be inferred.

We lived in a round of visits for some time after our return home, giving splendid dinner-parties, and making a sensation in our neighbourhood by the new lustre of our equipage, for my father had reserved this display of his increased wealth for the period of his son's marriage; and we gave our acquaintances liberal opportunity for remarking that it was a pity I made so poor a figure as an heir and a bridegroom. The nervous fatigue of this existence, the insincerities and platitudes which I had to live through twice over—through my inner and outward sense—would have been maddening to me, if I had not had that sort of intoxicated callousness which came from the delights of a first passion. A bride and bridegroom, surrounded by all the appliances of wealth, hurried through the day by the whirl of society, filling their solitary moments with hastily-snatched caresses, are prepared for their future life together as the novice is prepared for the cloister—by experiencing its utmost contrast.

Through all these crowded excited months, Bertha's inward self remained shrouded from me, and I still read her thoughts only through the language of her lips and demeanour: I had still the human interest of wondering whether what I did and said pleased her, of longing to hear a word of affection, of giving a delicious exaggeration of meaning to her smile. But I was conscious of a growing difference in her manner towards me; sometimes strong enough to be called haughty coldness, cutting and chilling me as the hail had done that came across the sunshine on our marriage morning; sometimes only perceptible in the dexterous avoidance of a tête-à-tête walk or dinner to which I had been looking forward. I had been deeply pained by this—had even felt a sort of crushing of the heart, from the sense that my brief day of happiness was near its setting; but still I remained dependent on Bertha, eager for the last rays of a bliss that would soon be gone for ever, hoping and watching for some after-glow more beautiful from the impending night.

I remember—how should I not remember?—the time when that dependence and hope utterly left me, when the sadness I had felt in Bertha's growing estrangement became a joy that I looked back upon with longing as a man might look back on the last pains in a paralysed limb. It was just after the close of my father's last illness, which had necessarily withdrawn us from society and thrown us more on each other. It was the evening of father's death. On that evening the veil which had shrouded Bertha's soul from me—had made me find in her alone among my fellow-beings the blessed possibility of mystery, and doubt, and expectation—was first withdrawn. Perhaps it was the first day since the beginning of my passion for her, in which that passion was completely neutralized by the presence of an absorbing feeling of another kind. I had been watching by my father's deathbed: I had been witnessing the last fitful yearning glance his soul had cast back on the spent inheritance of life—the last faint consciousness of love he had gathered from the pressure of my hand. What are all our personal loves when we have been sharing in that supreme agony? In the first moments when we come away from the presence of death, every other relation to the living is merged, to our feeling, in the great relation of a common nature and a common destiny.

In that state of mind I joined Bertha in her private sitting-room. She was seated in a leaning posture on a settee, with her back towards the door; the great rich coils of her pale blond hair surmounting her small neck, visible above the back of the settee. I remember, as I closed the door behind me, a cold tremulousness seizing me, and a vague sense of being hated and lonely—vague and strong, like a presentiment. I know how I looked at that moment, for I saw myself in Bertha's thought as she lifted her cutting grey eyes, and looked at me: a miserable ghost-seer, surrounded by phantoms in the noonday, trembling under a breeze when the leaves were still, without appetite for the common objects of human desires, but pining after the moon-beams. We were front to front with each other, and judged each other. The terrible moment of complete illumination had come to me, and I saw that the darkness had hidden no landscape from me, but only a blank prosaic wall: from that evening forth, through the sickening years which followed, I saw all round the narrow room of this woman's soul—saw petty artifice and mere negation where I had delighted to believe in coy sensibilities and in wit at war with latent feeling—saw the light floating vanities of the girl defining themselves into the systematic coquetry, the scheming selfishness, of the woman—saw repulsion and antipathy harden into cruel hatred, giving pain only for the sake of wreaking itself.

For Bertha too, after her kind, felt the bitterness of disillusion. She had believed that my wild poet's passion for her would make me her slave; and that, being her slave, I should execute her will in all things. With the essential shallowness of a negative, unimaginative nature, she was unable to conceive the fact that sensibilities were anything else than weaknesses. She had thought my weaknesses would put me in her power, and she found them unmanageable forces. Our positions were reversed. Before marriage she had completely mastered my imagination, for she was a secret to me; and I created the unknown thought before which I trembled as if it were hers. But now that her soul was laid open to me, now that I was compelled to share the privacy of her motives, to follow all the petty devices that preceded her words and acts, she found herself powerless with me, except to produce in me the chill shudder of repulsion—powerless, because I could be acted on by no lever within her reach. I was dead to worldly ambitions, to social vanities, to all the incentives within the compass of her narrow imagination, and I lived under influences utterly invisible to her.

She was really pitiable to have such a husband, and so all the world thought. A graceful, brilliant woman, like Bertha, who smiled on morning callers, made a figure in ball-rooms, and was capable of that light repartee which, from such a woman, is accepted as wit, was secure of carrying off all sympathy from a husband who was sickly, abstracted, and, as some suspected, crack-brained. Even the servants in our house gave her the balance of their regard and pity. For there were no audible quarrels between us; our alienation, our repulsion from each other, lay within the silence of our own hearts; and if the mistress went out a great deal, and seemed to dislike the master's society, was it not natural, poor thing? The master was odd. I was kind and just to my dependants, but I excited in them a shrinking, half-contemptuous pity; for this class of men and women are but slightly determined in their estimate of others by general considerations, or even experience, of character. They judge of persons as they judge of coins, and value those who pass current at a high rate.

After a time I interfered so little with Bertha's habits that it might seem wonderful how her hatred towards me could grow so intense and active as it did. But she had begun to suspect, by some involuntary betrayal of mine, that there was an abnormal power of penetration in me—that fitfully, at least, I was strangely cognizant of her thoughts and intentions, and she began to be haunted by a terror of me, which alternated every now and then with defiance. She meditated continually how the incubus could be shaken off her life—how she could be freed from this hateful bond to a being whom she at once despised as an imbecile, and dreaded as an inquisitor. For a long while she lived in the hope that my evident wretchedness would drive me to the commission of suicide; but suicide was not in my nature. I was too completely swayed by the sense that I was in the grasp of unknown forces, to believe in my power of self-release. Towards my own destiny I had become entirely passive; for my one ardent desire had spent itself, and impulse no longer predominated over knowledge. For this reason I never thought of taking any steps towards a complete separation, which would have made our alienation evident to the world. Why should I rush for help to a new course, when I was only suffering from the consequences of a deed which had been the act of my intensest will? That would have been the logic of one who had desires to gratify, and I had no desires. But Bertha and I lived more and more aloof from each other. The rich find it easy to live married and apart.

That course of our life which I have indicated in a few sentences filled the space of years. So much misery—so slow and hideous a growth of hatred and sin, may be compressed into a sentence! And men judge of each other's lives through this summary medium. They epitomize the experience of their fellow-mortal, and pronounce judgment on him in neat syntax, and feel themselves wise and virtuous—conquerors over the temptations they define in well-selected predicates. Seven years of wretchedness glide glibly over the lips of the man who has never counted them out in moments of chill disappointment, of head and heart throbbings, of dread and vain wrestling, of remorse and despair. We learn words by rote, but not their meaning; thatmust be paid for with our life-blood, and printed in the subtle fibres of our nerves.

But I will hasten to finish my story. Brevity is justified at once to those who readily understand, and to those who will never understand.

Some years after my father's death, I was sitting by the dim firelight in my library one January evening—sitting in the leather chair that used to be my father's—when Bertha appeared at the door, with a candle in her hand, and advanced towards me. I knew the ball-dress she had on—the white ball-dress, with the green jewels, shone upon by the light of the wax candle which lit up the medallion of the dying Cleopatra on the mantelpiece. Why did she come to me before going out? I had not seen her in the library, which was my habitual place for months. Why did she stand before me with the candle in her hand, with her cruel contemptuous eyes fixed on me, and the glittering serpent, like a familiar demon, on her breast? For a moment I thought this fulfilment of my vision at Vienna marked some dreadful crisis in my fate, but I saw nothing in Bertha's mind, as she stood before me, except scorn for the look of overwhelming misery with which I sat before her . . . "Fool, idiot, why don't you kill yourself, then?"— that was her thought. But at length her thoughts reverted to her errand, and she spoke aloud. The apparently indifferent nature of the errand seemed to make a ridiculous anticlimax to my prevision and my agitation.

"I have had to hire a new maid. Fletcher is going to be married, and she wants me to ask you to let her husband have the public-house and farm at Molton. I wish him to have it. You must give the promise now, because Fletcher is going to-morrow morning—and quickly, because I'm in a hurry."

"Very well; you may promise her," I said, indifferently, and Bertha swept out of the library again.

I always shrank from the sight of a new person, and all the more when it was a person whose mental life was likely to weary my reluctant insight with worldly ignorant trivialities. But I shrank especially from the sight of this new maid, because her advent had been announced to me at a moment to which I could not cease to attach some fatality: I had a vague dread that I should find her mixed up with the dreary drama of my life—that some new sickening vision would reveal her to me as an evil genius. When at last I did unavoidably meet her, the vague dread was changed into definite disgust. She was a tall, wiry, dark-eyed woman, this Mrs. Archer, with a face handsome enough to give her coarse hard nature the odious finish of bold, self-confident coquetry. That was enough to make me avoid her, quite apart from the contemptuous feeling with which she contemplated me. I seldom saw her; but I perceived that she rapidly became a favourite with her mistress, and, after the lapse of eight or nine months, I began to be aware that there had arisen in Bertha's mind towards this woman a mingled feeling of fear and dependence, and that this feeling was associated with ill-defined images of candle-light scenes in her dressing-room, and the locking-up of something in Bertha's cabinet. My interviews with my wife had become so brief and so rarely solitary, that I had no opportunity of perceiving these images in her mind with more definiteness. The recollections of the past become contracted in the rapidity of thought till they sometimes bear hardly a more distinct resemblance to the external reality than the forms of an oriental alphabet to the objects that suggested them.

Besides, for the last year or more a modification had been going forward in my mental condition, and was growing more and more marked. My insight into the minds of those around me was becoming dimmer and more fitful, and the ideas that crowded my double consciousness became less and less dependent on any personal contact. All that was personal in me seemed to be suffering a gradual death, so that I was losing the organ through which the personal agitations and projects of others could affect me. But along with this relief from wearisome insight, there was a new development of what I concluded—as I have since found rightly—to be a provision of external scenes. It was as if the relation between me and my fellow-men was more and more deadened, and my relation to what we call the inanimate was quickened into new life. The more I lived apart from society, and in proportion as my wretchedness subsided from the violent throb of agonized passion into the dulness of habitual pain, the more frequent and vivid became such visions as that I had had of Prague—of strange cities, of sandy plains, of gigantic ruins, of midnight skies with strange bright constellations, of mountain-passes, of grassy nooks flecked with the afternoon sunshine through the boughs: I was in the midst of such scenes, and in all of them one presence seemed to weigh on me in all these mighty shapes—the presence of something unknown and pitiless. For continual suffering had annihilated religious faith within me: to the utterly miserable—the unloving and the unloved—there is no religion possible, no worship but a worship of devils. And beyond all these, and continually recurring, was the vision of my death—the pangs, the suffocation, the last struggle, when life would be grasped at in vain.

Things were in this state near the end of the seventh year. I had become entirely free from insight, from my abnormal cognizance of any other consciousness than my own, and instead of intruding involuntarily into the world of other minds, was living continually in my own solitary future. Bertha was aware that I was greatly changed. To my surprise she had of late seemed to seek opportunities of remaining in my society, and had cultivated that kind of distant yet familiar talk which is customary between a husband and wife who live in polite and irrevocable alienation. I bore this with languid submission, and without feeling enough interest in her motives to be roused into keen observation; yet I could not help perceiving something triumphant and excited in her carriage and the expression of her face—something too subtle to express itself in words or tones, but giving one the idea that she lived in a state of expectation or hopeful suspense. My chief feeling was satisfaction that her inner self was once more shut out from me; and I almost revelled for the moment in the absent melancholy that made me answer her at cross purposes, and betray utter ignorance of what she had been saying. I remember well the look and the smile with which she one day said, after a mistake of this kind on my part: "I used to think you were a clairvoyant, and that was the reason why you were so bitter against other clairvoyants, wanting to keep your monopoly; but I see now you have become rather duller than the rest of the world."

I said nothing in reply. It occurred to me that her recent obtrusion of herself upon me might have been prompted by the wish to test my power of detecting some of her secrets; but I let the thought drop again at once: her motives and her deeds had no interest for me, and whatever pleasures she might be seeking, I had no wish to baulk her. There was still pity in my soul for every living thing, and Bertha was living—was surrounded with possibilities of misery.

Just at this time there occurred an event which roused me somewhat from my inertia, and gave me an interest in the passing moment that I had thought impossible for me. It was a visit from Charles Meunier, who had written me word that he was coming to England for relaxation from too strenuous labour, and would like too see me. Meunier had now a European reputation; but his letter to me expressed that keen remembrance of an early regard, an early debt of sympathy, which is inseparable from nobility of character: and I too felt as if his presence would be to me like a transient resurrection into a happier pre-existence.

He came, and as far as possible, I renewed our old pleasure of making tête-à-tête excursions, though, instead of mountains and glacers and the wide blue lake, we had to content ourselves with mere slopes and ponds and artificial plantations. The years had changed us both, but with what different result! Meunier was now a brilliant figure in society, to whom elegant women pretended to listen, and whose acquaintance was boasted of by noblemen ambitious of brains. He repressed with the utmost delicacy all betrayal of the shock which I am sure he must have received from our meeting, or of a desire to penetrate into my condition and circumstances, and sought by the utmost exertion of his charming social powers to make our reunion agreeable. Bertha was much struck by the unexpected fascinations of a visitor whom she had expected to find presentable only on the score of his celebrity, and put forth all her coquetries and accomplishments. Apparently she succeeded in attracting his admiration, for his manner towards her was attentive and flattering. The effect of his presence on me was so benignant, especially in those renewals of our old tête-à-tête wanderings, when he poured forth to me wonderful narratives of his professional experience, that more than once, when his talk turned on the psychological relations of disease, the thought crossed my mind that, if his stay with me were long enough, I might possibly bring myself to tell this man the secrets of my lot. Might there not lie some remedy for me, too, in his science? Might there not at least lie some comprehension and sympathy ready for me in his large and susceptible mind? But the thought only flickered feebly now and then, and died out before it could become a wish. The horror I had of again breaking in on the privacy of another soul, made me, by an irrational instinct, draw the shroud of concealment more closely around my own, as we automatically perform the gesture we feel to be wanting in another.

When Meunier's visit was approaching its conclusion, there happened an event which caused some excitement in our household, owing to the surprisingly strong effect it appeared to produce on Bertha—on Bertha, the self-possessed, who usually seemed inaccessible to feminine agitations, and did even her hate in a self-restrained hygienic manner. This event was the sudden severe illness of her maid, Mrs. Archer. I have reserved to this moment the mention of a circumstance which had forced itself on my notice shortly before Meunier's arrival, namely, that there had been some quarrel between Bertha and this maid, apparently during a visit to a distant family, in which she had accompanied her mistress. I had overheard Archer speaking in a tone of bitter insolence, which I should have thought an adequate reason for immediate dismissal. No dismissal followed; on the contrary, Bertha seemed to be silently putting up with personal inconveniences from the exhibitions of this woman's temper. I was the more astonished to observe that her illness seemed a cause of strong solicitude to Bertha; that she was at the bedside night and day, and would allow no one else to officiate as head-nurse. It happened that our family doctor was out on a holiday, an accident which made Meunier's presence in the house doubly welcome, and he apparently entered into the case with an interest which seemed so much stronger than the ordinary professional feeling, that one day when he had fallen into a long fit of silence after visiting her, I said to him—

"Is this a very peculiar case of disease, Meunier?"

"No," he answered, "it is an attack of peritonitis, which will be fatal, but which does not differ physically from many other cases that have come under my observation. But I'll tell you what I have on my mind. I want to make an experiment on this woman, if you will give me permission. It can do her no harm—will give her no pain—for I shall not make it until life is extinct to all purposes of sensation. I want to try the effect of transfusing blood into her arteries after the heart has ceased to beat for some minutes. I have tried the experiment again and again with animals that have died of this disease, with astounding results, and I want to try it on a human subject. I have the small tubes necessary, in a case I have with me, and the rest of the apparatus could be prepared readily. I should use my own blood—take it from my own arm. This woman won't live through the night, I'm convinced, and I want you to promise me your assistance in making the experiment. I can't do without another hand, but it would perhaps not be well to call in a medical assistant from among your provincial doctors. A disagreeable foolish version of the thing might get abroad."

"Have you spoken to my wife on the subject?" I said, "because she appears to be peculiarly sensitive about this woman: she has been a favourite maid."

"To tell you the truth," said Meunier, "I don't want her to know about it. There are always insuperable difficulties with women in these matters, and the effect on the supposed dead body may be startling. You and I will sit up

99

together, and be in readiness. When certain symptoms appear I shall take you in, and at the right moment we must manage to get every one else out of the room."

I need not give our farther conversation on the subject. He entered very fully into the details, and overcame my repulsion from them, by exciting in me a mingled awe and curiosity concerning the possible results of his experiment. We prepared everything, and he instructed me in my part as assistant. He had not told Bertha of his absolute conviction that Archer would not survive through the night, and endeavoured to persuade her to leave the patient and take a night's rest. But she was obstinate, suspecting the fact that death was at hand, and supposing that he wished merely to save her nerves. She refused to leave the sickroom. Meunier and I sat up together in the library, he making frequent visits to the sick-room, and returning with the information that the case was taking precisely the course he expected. Once he said to me, "Can you imagine any cause of ill-feeling this woman has against her mistress, who is so devoted to her?" "I think there was some misunderstanding between them before her illness. Why do you ask?"

"Because I have observed for the last five or six hours—since, I fancy, she has lost all hope of recovery—there seems a strange prompting in her to say something which pain and failing strength forbid her to utter; and there is a look of hideous meaning in her eyes, which she turns continually towards her mistress. In this disease the mind often remains singularly clear to the last."

"I am not surprised at an indication of malevolent feeling in her," I said. "She is a woman who has always inspired me with distrust and dislike, but she managed to insinuate herself into her mistress's favour." He was silent after this, looking at the fire with an air of absorption, till he went upstairs again. He stayed away longer than usual, and on returning, said to me quietly, "Come now."

I followed him to the chamber where death was hovering. The dark hangings of the large bed made a background that gave a strong relief to Bertha's pale face as I entered. She started forward as she saw me enter, and then looked at Meunier with an expression of angry inquiry; but he lifted up his hand as it to impose silence, while he fixed his glance on the dying woman and felt her pulse. The face was pinched and ghastly, a cold perspiration was on the forehead, and the eyelids were lowered so as to conceal the large dark eyes. After a minute or two, Meunier walked round to the other side of the bed where Bertha stood, and with his usual air of gentle politeness towards her begged her to leave the patient under our care—everything should be done for her—she was no longer in a state to be conscious of an affectionate presence. Bertha was hesitating, apparently almost willing to believe his assurance and to comply. She looked round at the ghastly dying face, as if to read the confirmation of that assurance, when for a moment the lowered eyelids were raised again, and it seemed as if the eyes were looking towards Bertha, but blankly. A shudder passed through Bertha's frame, and she returned to her station near the pillow, tacitly implying that she would not leave the room.

The eyelids were lifted no more. Once I looked at Bertha as she watched the face of the dying one. She wore a rich peignoir, and her blond hair was half covered by a lace cap: in her attire she was, as always, an elegant woman, fit to figure in a picture of modern aristocratic life: but I asked myself how that face of hers could ever have seemed to me the face of a woman born of woman, with memories of childhood, capable of pain, needing to be fondled? The features at that moment seemed so preternaturally sharp, the eyes were so hard and eager—she looked like a cruel immortal, finding her spiritual feast in the agonies of a dying race. For across those hard features there came something like a flash when the last hour had been breathed out, and we all felt that the dark veil had completely fallen. What secret was there between Bertha and this woman? I turned my eyes from her with a horrible dread lest my insight should return, and I should be obliged to see what had been breeding about two unloving women's hearts. I felt that Bertha had been watching for the moment of death as the sealing of her secret: I thanked Heaven it could remain sealed for me.

Meunier said quietly, "She is gone." He then gave his arm to Bertha, and she submitted to be led out of the room.

I suppose it was at her order that two female attendants came into the room, and dismissed the younger one who had been present before. When they entered, Meunier had already opened the artery in the long thin neck that lay rigid on the pillow, and I dismissed them, ordering them to remain at a distance till we rang: the doctor, I said, had an operation to perform—he was not sure about the death. For the next twenty minutes I forgot everything but Meunier and the experiment in which he was so absorbed, that I think his senses would have been closed against all sounds or sights which had no relation to it. It was my task at first to keep up the artificial respiration in the body after the transfusion had been effected, but presently Meunier relieved me, and I could see the wondrous slow return of life; the breast began to heave, the inspirations became stronger, the eyelids quivered, and the soul seemed to have returned beneath them. The artificial respiration was withdrawn: still the breathing continued, and there was a movement of the lips.

Just then I heard the handle of the door moving: I suppose Bertha had heard from the women that they had been dismissed: probably a vague fear had arisen in her mind, for she entered with a look of alarm. She came to the foot of the bed and gave a stifled cry.

The dead woman's eyes were wide open, and met hers in full recognition—the recognition of hate. With a sudden strong effort, the hand that Bertha had thought for ever still was pointed towards her, and the haggard face moved. The gasping eager voice said—

"You mean to poison your husband . . . the poison is in the black cabinet . . . I got it for you . . . you laughed at me, and told lies about me behind my back, to make me disgusting . . . because you were jealous . . . are you sorry . . . now?"

The lips continued to murmur, but the sounds were no longer distinct. Soon there was no sound—only a slight movement: the flame had leaped out, and was being extinguished the faster. The wretched woman's heart-strings had been set to hatred and vengeance; the spirit of life had swept the chords for an instant, and was gone again for ever. Great God! Is this what it is to live again... to wake up with our unstilled thirst upon us, with our unuttered curses rising to our lips, with our muscles ready to act out their half-committed sins?

Bertha stood pale at the foot of the bed, quivering and helpless, despairing of devices, like a cunning animal whose hiding-places are surrounded by swift-advancing flame. Even Meunier looked paralysed; life for that moment ceased to be a scientific problem to him. As for me, this scene seemed of one texture with the rest of my existence: horror was my familiar, and this new revelation was only like an old pain recurring with new circumstances.

* * * * *

Since then Bertha and I have lived apart—she in her own neighbourhood, the mistress of half our wealth, I as a wanderer in foreign countries, until I came to this Devonshire nest to die. Bertha lives pitied and admired; for what had I against that charming woman, whom every one but myself could have been happy with? There had been no witness of the scene in the dying room except Meunier, and while Meunier lived his lips were sealed by a promise to me.

Once or twice, weary of wandering, I rested in a favourite spot, and my heart went out towards the men and women and children whose faces were becoming familiar to me; but I was driven away again in terror at the approach of my old insight—driven away to live continually with the one Unknown Presence revealed and yet hidden by the moving curtain of the earth and sky. Till at last disease took hold of me and forced me to rest here—forced me to live in dependence on my servants. And then the curse of insight—of my double consciousness, came again, and has never left me. I know all their narrow thoughts, their feeble regard, their half-wearied pity.

* * * * *

It is the 20th of September, 1850. I know these figures I have just written, as if they were a long familiar inscription. I have seen them on this pace in my desk unnumbered times, when the scene of my dying struggle has opened upon me...

102

Appendix

Bates, Arlo and Eleanor Putnam. "Old Salem" Boston: Houghton Mifflin Company, 1886. Internet Archive.

Bell, Acton, Currer Bell and Ellis Bell. *Poems by Currer, Ellis, and Acton Bell.* London: Aylott & Jones, 1846. Project Gutenberg.

Carroll, Lewis. "The Hunting of the Snark" London: Macmillan Publishers, 1876. Project Gutenberg.

Dickens, Charles. *Sketches by Boz.* London: James Macrone, St. James Square, 1836. Project Gutenberg.

Eliot, George. *The Lifted Veil.* Edinburgh: Blackwood's Magazine, 1859. Project Gutenberg.

Fleming, William F. "The Good Brahmin" Akron, OH: The Werner Company, 1906. Translation. Wikisource.

Franklin, Benjamin. "Silence Dogood No. 1, 2 April 1722" *The New England Courant*, 1722. Founders Online. National Archives.

Henry, O. "The Trimmed Lamp." Garden City, NY: Doubleday, Page & Co., 1914. Project Gutenberg.

Russell, George William. *The Nuts of Knowledge.* Dublin: Dun Emer Press, 1903. Project Gutenberg.

Seltzer, Thomas. *Best Russian Short Stories.* New York City: Boni & Liveright Inc., 1917. Wikisource.

Twain, Mark. "A Dog's Tale" New York City: Harper & Brothers, 1904. Project Gutenberg.

Portraits

"Anne Brontë." Wikipedia, Wikimedia Foundation, 9 Oct. 2018, en.wikipedia. org/wiki/Anne_Bront%C3%AB.

"Anton Chekhov 1904." Wikimedia Commons. January 1, 2010. https://commons.wikimedia.org/wiki/File:Anton_Chekhov_1904.JPG.

"Franklin-Benjamin-LOC." Wikimedia Commons. October 23, 2008. https:// commons.wikimedia.org/wiki/File:Franklin-Benjamin-LOC.jpg.

"Dickens Gurney Head." Wikimedia Commons. August 29, 2014. https://commons.wikimedia.org/wiki/File:Dickens_Gurney_head.jpg.

"Charlotte Brontë." Wikimedia Commons. June 11, 2005. https://commons. wikimedia.org/wiki/File:Charlotte_Brontë.jpg

"Emily Brontë." Wikipedia. November 07, 2018. https://en.wikipedia.org/wiki/ Emily_Brontë#/media/File:Emily_Brontë_by_Patrick_Branwell_Brontë_restored.jpg.

"George Eliot." Wikipedia, Wikimedia Foundation, 20 Oct. 2018, en.wikipedia. org/wiki/George_Eliot.

"George William Russell." Wikipedia, Wikimedia Foundation, 21 Oct. 2018, en.wikipedia.org/wiki/George_William_Russell.

"Harriet Bates." Wikipedia, Wikimedia Foundation, 28 Sept. 2018, en.wikipedia. org/wiki/Harriet_Bates.

"Lewis Carroll." Wikipedia, Wikimedia Foundation, 17 Oct. 2018, en.wikipedia. org/wiki/Lewis_Carroll.

"Mark Twain." Wikipedia, Wikimedia Foundation, 19 Oct. 2018, en.wikipedia. org/wiki/Mark_Twain.

"Picture of O. Henry." Wikimedia Commons. October 29, 2016. https://commons.wikimedia.org/wiki/File:Picture_of_O._Henry.jpg.

"Nicolas De Largillière, François-Marie Arouet Dit Voltaire." Wikimedia Commons. July 18, 2017. https://commons.wikimedia.org/wiki/File:Nicolas_de_Largilli%C3%A8re,_Fran%C3%A7ois-Marie_Arouet_dit_Voltaire_(vers_1724-1725)_-001.jpg

www.ingramcontent.com/pod-product-compliance
Lightning Source LLC
Chambersburg PA
CBHW021122130626
46554CB00002B/815